DEPARTMENT OF HEALTH

The Children Act Guidance and Regulations

Volume 1
Court Orders

A NEW FRAMEWORK FOR THE CARE
AND UPBRINGING OF CHILDREN

LONDON: HMSO

© Crown copyright 1991
First published 1991
ISBN 0 11 321371 9

ii

Preface

This guidance is Handbook is issued under section 7 of the Local Authority Social Services Act 1970. It is the first in a series of such books designed to bring to managers and practitioners an understanding of the principles of the Children Act and associated regulations, to identify areas of change and to discuss the implications for policies, procedures and practice. It is not intended that any one handbook should be read as a discrete entity. The Children Act was conceived as a cohesive legal framework for the care and protection of children. Each volume of guidance should therefore be read in conjunction with the others in the series and cross-references are made where appropriate. The need to build on sound practice and the multi-agency, multi-disciplinary co-operation identified in Working Together and the Principles and Practice Guide is also reinforced throughout the Act.

The guidance is written as if the Children Act is currently in force and refers in the past tense to legislation which is repealed by the Act and guidance which is withdrawn in consequence. A glossary of terms and index will be provided for the guidance as a whole.

Contents

4   PROTECTION OF CHILDREN   44

CHAPTER 1   INTRODUCTION

1.1. The Children Act 1989 brings together in a single coherent legislative framework the private and public law relating to children. It aims to strike a balance between the rights of children to express their views on decisions made about their lives, the rights of parents to exercise their responsibilities towards the child and the duty of the state to intervene where the child's welfare requires it.

1.2. The courts have considerable scope for discretion in their decisions about children. It is therefore important that practitioners in the field understand the broad objectives which the legislation aims to achieve and the tools which it employs to do so.

1.3. This volume of guidance considers the major new orders available under Parts I, II, IV and V of the Act as well as secure accommodation orders (Part III, section 25) and the criminal implications of the Children Act contained in Part XII and schedule 12. Guidance on education supervision orders is produced separately by the Department of Education and Science.

1.4. As with much else in the Act, court orders cannot be seen as a free-standing end product but must be considered within the context of a wide range of provisions available under the Act. It is therefore intended that this guidance be read in conjunction with the other volumes of guidance and Regulations in this series and in particular guidance on the cornerstone provisions of services for families with children in need contained in Part III of the Act.

Children and their families

1.5. The Children Act rests on the belief that children are generally best looked after within the family with both parents playing a full part and without resort to legal proceedings. That belief, further explored and translated into practice in Volume 2, is reflected in:

(a) the new concept of parental responsibility;

(b) the ability of unmarried fathers to share that responsibility by agreement with the mother;

(c) the local authority's duty to give support to children and their families;

(d) the local authority's duty to return a child looked after by them to his family unless this is against his interests;

(e) the local authority's duty to ensure contact with his parents whenever possible for a child looked after by them away from home.

Child-centred welfare principles

1.6. The opening provisions of the Act set out the overarching welfare principles to be applied in all proceedings under the Act.

1.7. In deciding any question about a child's upbringing and administration of his property the court must treat the welfare of the child as the paramount consideration. This applies equally to care proceedings and emergency protection proceedings as it does to disputes between parents.

1.8. The Act makes it clear that delay in court proceedings is generally harmful to children not only because of the uncertainty it creates for them but also because of the harm it does to the relationship between the parents and their capacity to co-operate with one another in the future. Progress of a case is therefore to be controlled by the court (rather than the parties) which will be required to draw up a timetable and take appropriate measures to reduce delay to a minimum.

1.9. In contested family proceedings and in all care and supervision proceedings the court, when applying the welfare principle, should have regard to the following checklist of factors which focuses not only on the needs of the child but also on his views and the options available to the court:

(a) the ascertainable wishes and feelings of the child concerned (considered in the light of his age and understanding);

(b) his physical, emotional and educational needs;

(c) the likely effect on him of any change in his circumstances;

(d) his age, sex, background and any characteristics of his which the court considers relevant;

(e) any harm which he has suffered or is at risk of suffering;

(f) how capable each of his parents and any other person in relation to whom the court considers the question to be relevant, is of meeting his needs;

(g) the range or powers available to the court under this Act in the proceedings in question.

1.10. The checklist makes it clear that, whatever the order applied for in private proceedings, the court may make any other private order if it thinks it is best for the child, or may trigger a local authority investigation to see whether the authority should apply for one of the orders available to protect the child. The full range of orders is also available to a court hearing a local authority application for a care or other order in respect of the child.

1.11. The Act prohibits the court from making an order unless it is satisfied that the order will positively contribute to the child's welfare.

1.12. There are two aims. The first is to discourage unnecessary court orders being made, for example as part of a standard package of orders. If orders are restricted to those cases where they are necessary to resolve a specific problem this should reduce conflict and promote parental agreement and co-operation. The second aim is to ensure that the order is granted only where it will positively improve the child's welfare and not simply because the grounds for making the order are made out as, for example, in care proceedings where the court may decide that it would be better for a particular child not to be in local authority care.

Concurrent system of jurisdiction

1.13. The Children Act creates a concurrent system of jurisdiction for a wide range of family proceedings in new magistrates' family proceedings courts, county courts and the High Court. Rules governing the allocation and transfer of cases either vertically between the various tiers, or horizontally within tiers, will ensure that cases are directed to the most appropriate court.

1.14. In practice the majority of public law cases will be heard entirely in the magistrates' family proceedings court as usually this will be the most appropriate court. Different considerations apply to private law cases where for the time being it will continue to be possible to exercise free choice about which court is used.

1.15. Most public law applications will start in the magistrates' family proceedings court but in certain circumstances can be transferred to a higher court. Subject to the overriding principle that delay is likely to prejudice the welfare of the child the criteria for transfer are:

(a) exceptional complexity, importance or gravity;

(b) the need to consolidate with other proceedings;

(c) urgency.

Appeals

1.16. There is a general right of appeal to the High Court against both the making of and refusal to make any order. The major exception is that there can be no appeal against the making of or refusal to make an emergency protection order nor against any associated order or direction as, for example, the discharge of the order or its extension. The Act introduces three important changes insofar as appeals in care proceedings are concerned, namely:

(a) appeals lie to the High Court and not the Crown Court, thereby reinforcing the civil nature of such applications;

(b) appeals lie against the refusal as well as the making of a care or supervision order;

(c) the local authority and parents will have full rights of appeal.

As before, appeals against decisions made in the county or High Court may lie to the Court of Appeal.

Non-adversarial stance

1.17. The rules of court which regulate the proceedings across all three tiers of jurisdiction have been designed to promote a non-adversarial style in court. The complaint/summons procedure has been abandoned in favour of the commencement of proceedings by application. For the first time a directions appointment is introduced to both public and private law proceedings as a preliminary hearing at which, among other matters, timetables can be set, a guardian *ad litem* appointed in certain specified proceedings and evidential matters likely to be agreed or in dispute identified. These preliminary hearings should serve to minimise delay and produce less adversarial conduct of cases in court.

1.18. To facilitate ease of transfer between different jurisdictional tiers and to encourage the preparation of documentary evidence and advance disclosure, applications for most public and private law orders will be by way of prescribed forms. Applicants will be required to give a considerable amount of information as to the nature of their case, the order and any accompanying directions sought and, where relevant, their future plans for the child.

Role of the guardian *ad litem*

1.19. The Act enhances the role of the guardian *ad litem* in public law proceedings. The requirement to appoint a guardian *ad litem* has been strengthened by extending it to a wider range of proceedings, including in particular applications for emergency protection orders. In practice this is likely to mean that a guardian *ad litem* is appointed in every public law case unless the court is satisfied that it is unnecessary to do so to safeguard the interests of the child. Guardians *ad litem* will also be appointed earlier in the proceedings, so that they can play a full and active role not only as representative and spokesperson for the child but advising the court on matters such as timetabling and directions. The duties and functions of the guardian *ad litem* are prescribed by the rules of court and are considered more fully in the guidance on the administration and management of guardian *ad litem* panels.

Arrangement of the guidance

1.20. The chapters in this guidance follow broadly the relevant sections of the Act. Chapter 2 considers the major changes in private law relating to children under Parts I and II. A range of new and flexible orders, incorporating the more valuable features of the wardship jurisdiction, are introduced. These focus on the child's interests and the need to resolve specific areas of dispute. The orders will settle particular matters which neither party can upset. They will be made principally in private family proceedings but may also be made in care proceedings. Local authorities will need to be aware of the range of private law orders available and the circumstances in which they are likely to be used to safeguard and promote a child's welfare.

1.21. Parts IV and V of the Act establish a quite new legal framework for compulsory intervention in the care, supervision and protection of children at risk. Their implications are considerable, not only for the children concerned but also for their parents and others connected with the child and the responsibilities given to the courts, local authorities and others. Many provisions are radically different replacements of requirements in legislation repealed by the Act or are completely new. The preconditions for making a care order are rationalised and the basis for statutory intervention is directed towards the occurrence of present or future harm to the child. Chapter 3 deals with care and supervision orders and the implication of the Act on the use of wardship and the wider inherent jurisdiction of the High Court in public proceedings.

1.22. The law on the protection of children is discussed in Chapter 4. It fundamentally recasts the existing statutory provisions and establishes a system of checks and balances so as to ensure effective protective action can be taken while affording adequate safeguards and reasonable opportunities for those closely connected with the child to challenge such action before the court. Two new protection orders are introduced which are short-term and time limited and may or may not lead to action under parts III and IV of the Act.

1.23. Chapter 5 considers the basic statutory framework in the Children Act governing the restriction of liberty of children being looked after by local authorities and how this protection is extended to children in other types of accommodation. Fuller guidance on 'good practice' issues and case management of a child in secure accommodation is to be found in Volume 4 in this series.

1.24. The Act contains various provisions relating to juveniles who are at risk of committing offences or who have been accused or convicted of a criminal offence. Local authorities are under a new duty to take reasonable steps designed to reduce the need to bring criminal proceedings against juveniles in their area and to encourage them not to commit offences. The criminal care order is abolished and the courts are given a new power to attach residence requirements to criminal supervision orders. These and other implications of the Children Act for juvenile offending are discussed in Chapter 6.

1.25. The Act will be implemented as a whole on 14 October 1991. The Annex to this guidance sets out the transitional arrangements in relation to court orders that will come into effect on that day. In the run up to implementation and as soon afterwards as is reasonably practical local authorities should carefully consider whether any of the care and supervision orders likely to come into force as a result of these transitional arrangements should be varied or discharged. The new range of orders available under the Act and the duty of the local authority to provide services for families with children in need may suggest some lesser intervention consistent with that authority's duty to safeguard and promote the welfare of children currently in their care and this should be actively pursued.

CHAPTER 2 **PRIVATE LAW ASPECTS OF THE CHILDREN ACT**

2.1. The Children Act 1989 makes major changes in the private law relating to children. Part I of the Act introduces the fundamental concept of 'parental responsibility' to replace that of parental 'rights and duties' and creates a clear distinction between parenthood and guardianship, the latter being generally reserved for non-parents appointed to bring up a child on the death of his parents. Under Part II of the Act the courts are given power to make a range of new and flexible orders in respect of children in 'family proceedings', as defined by the Act, which will replace orders for custody, access and custodianship and which should reduce the need to use the wardship jurisdiction. These orders focus on the child's interests so as to resolve specific areas of dispute rather than allocating legal rights and are designed to encourage both parents to maintain their involvement in the child's life. They will be made principally in private family proceedings but they may also be made in care proceedings. Indeed, it is availability of these orders in care proceedings which greatly increases the options open to the courts to make orders that best suit the needs of the child. Finally, the basis on which private law orders relating to children may be granted has also been radically reformed, with improved legal standing for unmarried fathers as well as for relatives and other non-parents.

PARENTAL RESPONSIBILITY

The meaning of parental responsibility

2.2. 'Parental responsibility' is defined by section 3 of the Act as "all the rights, duties, powers, responsibilities and authority which by law a parent of a child has in relation to a child and his property" (section 3(1); by section 3(2) this includes the powers of a guardian in looking after the child's property, for example by giving a valid receipt for a legacy). Parental responsibility is therefore concerned with bringing the child up, caring for him and making decisions about him, but does not affect the relationship of parent and child for other purposes. Thus, whether or not a parent has parental responsibility for a child does not affect any obligation towards the child, such as a statutory duty to maintain him (section 3(4)(a)), nor does it affect succession rights (section 3(4)(b)).

2.3. In reading any provision of the Act relating to a parent, therefore, it is important to note whether it applies to any parent (ie the mother or father of the child) or only to a parent with parental responsibility (ie the mother always but the father only if he has parental responsibility under the rules set out in paragraph 2.4 below).

The Allocation of parental responsibility: married and unmarried parents

2.4. If the child's father and mother were married to one another at the time of his birth, they each have parental responsibility for the child (section 2(1)); the same applies if they are or have been married to one another at any time since the child's conception (by virtue of section 1(2) and (4) of the Family Law Reform Act 1987). If the child's father and mother were not married to one another only the mother has parental responsibility automatically (section 2(2)). An unmarried father may, however, acquire parental responsibility in four different ways:

(a) by applying to the court for a parental responsibility order under section 4(1); as with a parental rights and duties order under section 4 of the Family Law Reform Act 1987, this places him in the same position as a married father, sharing parental responsibility with the mother;

(b) by having a residence order under section 8 (see paragraph 2.26 below) made in his favour; the court must then make a parental responsibility order as well (section 12(1)) and this order need not come to an end just because the residence order is changed (section 12(4)); once again, the order places him in the same position as a married father, sharing parental responsibility with the mother;

(c) by making an agreement with the mother under section 4(1), in such form and recorded in such a manner as may be prescribed by the Lord Chancellor in Regulations (section 4(2)): this is intended to convey to parents the importance and legal effect of such an agreement, which is the same as an order under section 4(1) and can only be brought to an end by a court order;

(d) by being appointed guardian, either by the mother or by a court, to assume parental responsibility after the mother's death.

2.5. If mother and father are living together in a stable relationship when the child is born, and wish to share responsibility for bringing him up, it may well be in the child's interests for them to make a section 4 agreement, provided that they both understand what it means. Unless and until the court brings it to an end, their position will be the same as if they had been married; thus, for example, the father's agreement to any adoption will be necessary, unless it can be dispensed with, and he will be able to remove the child from accommodation provided by a local authority under section 20. The mother may also feel that it is important for them to share responsibility in this way even if they are not living together.

2.6. If for any reason they are living apart, either when the child is born or subsequently, and the father obtains an order that the child is to live with him, then he will also obtain a parental responsibility order automatically. Given this rule, and the availability of parental responsibility agreements where the mother is happy to share responsibility with the father, cases in which it will be in the child's interests to make a parental responsibility order without also making a residence order in the father's favour may not be very common. An example might be where neither the mother nor the father was looking after the child, perhaps because he was in local authority accommodation or being looked after by another member of the family, and it was appropriate for both parents to have overall responsibility for him.

2.7. The cases in which it would be appropriate to appoint the father guardian are perhaps even less common. The mother might wish to do this in case she were to die prematurely, but in that case she might be equally happy to make an agreement to share responsibility with him during her lifetime. If the question of a court appointment arises after the mother's death, it would be more appropriate to make a parental responsibility order, which recognises, not only that he has parental responsibility, but also that he is the child's father.

2.8. Both an agreement and an order under section 4 can only be brought to an end by a court order. Any person who has parental responsibility for the child (which includes the father), or the child himself with leave of the court (which may only be granted if the court is satisfied that the child has sufficient understanding to make the application) (section 4(4)), may apply for the parental responsibility order or agreement to be brought to an end (section 4(3)). Otherwise a parental responsibility order or agreement will end automatically when the child reaches the age of eighteen (section 91(7) and (8)).

2.9. An unmarried father who does not have parental responsibility is nevertheless a 'parent' for the purposes of the Act. He therefore has the right of any other parent to apply to the courts for any type of order (section 10(4)) and is entitled to reasonable contact with a child in care (under section 34(1)). He is not, however, entitled to remove a child from accommodation provided under section 20, nor is his agreement required to the child's adoption.

Delegation of parental responsibility

2.10. Informal arrangements for the delegation of parental responsibility are covered by section 2(9), which provides that a person with parental responsibility cannot surrender or transfer any part of that responsibility to another, but may arrange for some or all of it to be met by one or more persons acting on his behalf. The person to whom responsibility is delegated may already have parental responsibility for the child, for example if he is the other parent (section 2(10)). Such an arrangement will not, however, affect any liability of a person with parental responsibility for the child for failure to meet that responsibility (section 2(11)). Thus, the Act recognises the right of parents to delegate responsibility for their child on a temporary basis, for example to a babysitter or for a school trip, but it will still be the parent's duty to ensure that the arrangements made for temporary care of the child are satisfactory. Otherwise, the parent may be guilty of an offence under section 1 of the Children and Young Persons Act 1933.

Responsibility of carers

2.11. The position of the temporary carer is clarified by section 3(5), which provides that a person who has care of the child but does not have parental responsibility may do "what is reasonable in all the circumstances of the case for the purpose of safeguarding or promoting the child's welfare" (section 3(5)). This will cover actions taken by people looking after a child who is being accommodated by a local authority under section 20, provided that these are reasonable in the circumstances. What is reasonable will depend upon the urgency and gravity of what is required and the extent to which it is practicable to consult a person with parental responsibility. Anyone who cares for a child is obliged by section 1 of the Children and Young Persons Act 1933 not to assault, ill-treat, neglect, abandon or expose the child in a manner likely to cause unnecessary suffering or injury to health.

2.12. The remaining provisions relating to the sharing of parental responsibility are dealt with below (paragraphs 2.24 – 2.26), in relation to the effect of residence orders.

GUARDIANSHIP

2.13. The Children Act replaces the previous law of guardianship with a new and simplified statutory code. The object now is to provide someone to take parental responsibility for a child whose parents have died. The concept of parental guardianship is therefore abolished (by section 2(4) and the repeal of section 3 of the Guardianship of Minors Act 1971). All guardians will be non-parents, apart from those exceptional cases in which an unmarried father is appointed guardian instead of being given parental responsibility under section 4 (see paragraph 2.7 above). A guardian must be an 'individual', ie a human person rather than a local authority, voluntary organisation or trust corporation. Once the appointment takes effect, the guardian will have the same parental responsibility as a natural parent (section 5(6)); it will no longer be possible to appoint a guardian who is responsible for the child's property but not for bringing him up (there is a power for rules of court to preserve the inherent power of the High Court to appoint a guardian of the child's estate in certain exceptional cases where the Official Solicitor acts at present, for example in handling criminal injuries compensation for children who have been abused by their parents, but this has not been exercised at present). A guardian may be appointed by any parent with parental responsibility, or by any guardian, or by a court. With one exception, however, a private appointment cannot take effect, nor can a court appointment be made, if the child still has a surviving parent with parental responsibility for him.

2.14. A court can appoint a guardian either on application or of its own motion in any family proceedings (section 5(1) and (2)). An appointment might therefore be made instead of, or even in addition to, a care order in care proceedings. However, the court only has power to appoint a guardian in two situations:

(a) where the child has no parent with parental responsibility for him, either because both parents have died, or because his mother has died and his father does not have parental responsibility; or

(b) where the child still has a parent with parental responsibility, but there was a residence order in force in favour of a parent or guardian who has died (and not also in favour of the surviving parent (section 5(9)); this is to cater for a child whose parents are separated when the parent with whom he is living dies; but even then, if there is no court order providing that the child is to live with only one of them, the survivor will assume sole responsibility for him.

2.15. If either of the above situations arises in relation to a child who is the subject of a care order, the local authority may wish to consider whether it would be in the child's interests for someone, perhaps a member of the family, to be appointed to take the place of the parent who has died. That person would share parental responsibility with the authority, subject to the care order, and would be entitled to reasonable contact with the child under section 34(1), to apply for the care order to be discharged under section 39(1), and to withhold agreement to the child's adoption unless this could be dispensed with on any of the usual grounds. For some children this could be a valuable way of demonstrating the continued commitment and concern of their extended family, even if for the time being they are to remain in local authority care.

2.16. For a child who is accommodated under section 20 when either of the situations set out in paragraph 2.14 arises, it may be even more beneficial for a guardian to be appointed, particularly if the threshhold criteria for making a care order do not exist. Even if they do, the authority may wish to consider whether appointing a guardian would serve the child's interests better than making a care order.

2.17. Guardians may also be appointed by any parent with parental responsibility (section 5(3)) and by guardians themselves (section 5(4)). These appointments only take effect in the situations where a court has power to make an appointment; ie when there is no surviving parent with parental responsibility or when the person making the appointment had a residence order in his favour immediately before his death (section 5(7)) unless the residence order was made in favour of a surviving parent as well (section 5(9)).

2.18. The formalities for the private appointment of a guardian (or guardians) have been considerably relaxed and it will no longer be necessary, although still possible, for the appointment to be made by deed or by will. Instead, an appointment will be valid provided it is in writing and is dated and signed by the person making the appointment. Alternatively, the person making the appointment may direct another person to sign on his behalf, provided this is done in his presence and in the presence of two witnesses who each attest the signature (section 5(5)). This is to cater for blind or physically disabled people who cannot write, but not for those who are absent or mentally incapacitated.

Revocation, disclaimer and termination

2.19. Section 6 governs the revocation, disclaimer and termination of guardianship. The basic principle is that any later private appointment revokes an earlier one made by the same person in respect of the same child, unless it is clear that the purpose was to appoint an additional rather than a substitute

---

*The appointment of a 'guardian' should not be confused with the appointment of a 'guardian *ad litem*' in public law proceedings.

guardian (section 6(1)). Any appointment made in a will or codicil is revoked if the will itself is revoked in accordance with the special rules relating to the revocation of wills (section 6(4)), but all appointments, however made, can also be revoked in the same simple way that an appointment can be made (section 6(2): see paragraph 2.18 above), and an appointment made in a document other than a will or codicil can be revoked by destroying the document with the intention of revoking the appointment (section 6(3)).

2.20. There is also a new right for a privately appointed guardian formally to disclaim his appointment by written instrument, signed by him and made within a reasonable time of his first knowing that the appointment has taken effect (section 6(5)). This disclaimer must be recorded in accordance with any Regulations made by the Lord Chancellor (section 6(6)).

2.21. Guardianship comes to an end automatically when the child reaches the age of eighteen (section 91(7) and (8)), whether the appointment was made by the court or privately. Any appointment may also be brought to an end by order of the court on the application of:

(a) any person, including a local authority, who has parental responsibility for the child;

(b) with leave, the child himself; or

(c) of the court's own motion in any family proceedings (section 6(7)).

SECTION 8 ORDERS

2.22. Section 8 creates four new types of order: contact orders, prohibited steps orders, residence orders and specific issue orders. These are defined by section 8(1) as follows:-

'a contact order' means an order requiring the person with whom a child lives, or is to live, to allow the child to visit or stay with the person named in the order, or for that person and the child to have contact with each other;

'a prohibited steps order' means an order that no step which could be taken by a parent in meeting his parental responsibility for a child, and which is of a kind specified in the order, shall be taken by any person without the consent of the court;

'a residence order' means an order settling the arrangements to be made as to the person with whom a child is to live; and

'a specific issue order' means an order giving directions for the purpose of determining a specific question which has arisen, or which may arise, in connection with any aspect of parental responsibility for a child.

Any of these orders, or any order varying or discharging such an order, is referred to in the Act as 'a section 8 order'. The court will be able to make a section 8 order either upon application or of its own motion (section 10(1)(a) and (b)), unlike care and supervision orders which may not be made of the court's own motion, except on an interim basis (section 38(1)). The court will also have power, when making any section 8 order, to include directions about how it is to be carried into effect, to impose conditions to be complied with (i) by any person in whose favour the order is made or (ii) a parent or (iii) a non-parent with parental responsibility or (iv) a person with whom the child is living, to specify the period of which the order, or any provision contained in it, will have effect, and to make such incidental, supplemental or consequential provision as the court thinks fit. This is to enable the new orders to be as flexible as possible and so reduce or remove the need to resort to wardship.

Residence orders

2.23. The residence order replaces the present custody order but differs in certain important respects, firstly because it is more flexible and will be able to accommodate various shared care arrangements and, secondly, because residence and parental responsibility are regarded as quite separate concepts.

The intention is that *both* parents should feel that they have a continuing role to play in relation to their children.

2.24. Section 2(5) provides that more than one person may have parental responsibility for a child at the same time and by section 2(6) a person with parental responsibility for a child does not lose it just because some other person subsequently acquires it. Thus, the making of a residence order in favour of one parent does not take away parental responsibility from the other. Nor do the parent or parents of a child lose parental responsibility when a third party who is neither parent nor guardian of the child acquires parental responsibility, as an individual through the making of a residence order in his or her favour (section 12(2)) or a local authority, through the making of a care order (section 33(3)) (although the latter also has the power to determine the extent to which a parent or guardian of the child may meet his parental responsibility for him once the child is in care (section 33(3)(b))).

2.25. It is provided by section 2(7) that, where parental responsibility is shared, each may act independently of the other in meeting that responsibility. Thus, although the making of a residence order in favour of one parent may curb the other parent's ability to act independently to the extent that in practice the day to day care of the child is largely controlled by the parent with whom the child lives, at least when the child is with the non-residential parent he or she may meet his or her parental responsibility to the full, without the need for consultation with the other parent. The only restrictions on this are that neither parent may act independently in matters where the consent of more than one person is expressly required by statute (section 2(7)), for example under section 1 of the Child Abduction Act 1984 in relation to removal of the child from the United Kingdom or under section 16 of the Adoption Act 1976 in relation to agreement to an adoption order; nor may either parent act in any way that is incompatible with any order made in respect of the child (section 2(8)). Thus, for example, one parent may not remove the child from the physical care of the parent (or indeed any other person) with whom the child is to live by virtue of a residence order but could take the same interest as any other parent in his child's education.

2.26. By section 12(2) the making of a residence order in favour of a person who is neither parent nor guardian of a child has the effect of conferring parental responsibility on him or her while the residence order remains in force. However, he or she, like a local authority with a care order in its favour (see section 33(6)), does not acquire the right to consent or refuse consent to the making of an application to free the child for adoption or to the making of an adoption order, or the right to appoint a guardian. By section 12(1), where a residence order is made in favour of an unmarried father the court must also make an order under section 4 giving him parental responsibility; under section 12(4), this must not be brought to an end while the residence order concerned remains in force. Indeed, if the residence order is subsequently discharged the order giving him parental responsibility will continue unless and until it is specifically revoked. In such cases it will usually be in the child's interests for his father to retain parental responsibility for him in just the same way that a married father does.

2.27. Another effect of a residence order is that no person may cause the child to be known by a new surname nor remove him from the United Kingdom without either the written consent of every person who has parental responsibility for him or the leave of the court (section 13(1)). This does not, however, prevent the person in whose favour the residence order has been made from removing the child for a period of less than one month (section 13(2)). There is no limit on the number of these short trips, however, and if the non-residential parent feels that the child is being taken out of the United Kingdom too frequently or that there is a danger of abduction he or she should seek a prohibited steps order.

2.28. A residence order may be made in favour of more than one person at the same time even though they do not live together, in which case the order may specify the periods during which the child is to live in the different households concerned (section 11(4)). A shared residence order could therefore be made where the child is to spend, for example, weekdays with one parent and weekends with the other or term time with one parent and school holidays with the other, or where the child is to spend large amounts of time with each parent. This latter arrangement was disapproved of by the Court of Appeal in *Riley* v *Riley* (1986) 2 FLR 429, which must now be taken to have been over-ruled by section 11(4), but it is not expected that it will become a common form of order, partly because most children will still need the stability of a single home, and partly because in the cases where shared care is appropriate there is less likely to be a need for the court to make any order at all. However, a shared care order has the advantage of being more realistic in those cases where the child is to spend considerable amounts of time with both parents, brings with it certain other benefits (including the right to remove the child from accommodation provided by a local authority under section 20), and removes any impression that one parent is good and responsible whereas the other parent is not.

Contact orders

2.29. Unlike the present access order, which normally provides for a parent to have access to the child, the new contact order provides for the child to visit or stay with the person named in the order. The emphasis has thus shifted from the adult to the child. The new order may provide for the child to have contact with *any* person, not just a parent, and more than one contact order may be made in respect of a child. 'Contact' may range from long or short visits to contact by letter or telephone. It is anticipated that the usual order will be for reasonable contact, although the court will be able to attach conditions or make directions under section 11(7) where necessary. Contact orders, like residence orders will lapse if the parents subsequently live together for a period of more than six months (section 11(5) and (6)).

2.30. Contact orders under section 8 must be distinguished from orders under section 34 for contact with a child in care. Section 8 contact orders cannot be made if the child is the subject of a care order, because in this case the local authority has a statutory duty to allow the child reasonable contact with his parents (whether or not they both have parental responsibility), any guardian, and any other person with whom the child was to live by virtue of a residence order in force immediately before the care order was made. Section 34 contact orders will therefore only be made if it is necessary to limit, remove or define such contact, or to provide for contact with some other person. In the case of private individuals, however, it may sometimes be necessary to order them to allow reasonable contact, as well as to define what contact is to be allowed in particularly difficult or contentious cases. Occasionally, this may be necessary where a child is being provided with accommodation under section 20 and a dispute arises as to the contact which the foster parent or children's home should allow. It should be noted that a section 8 contact order is a positive order in the sense that it requires contact to be allowed between an individual and a child and cannot be used to deny contact. This would require a prohibited steps order.

Prohibited steps orders

2.31. Both prohibited steps orders and specific issues orders are concerned with 'single issues' and are modelled on the wardship jurisdiction. The purpose of the prohibited steps order, however, is to impose a *specific* restriction on the exercise of parental responsibility instead of the vague requirement in wardship that no 'important step' be taken in respect of the child without the court's consent. It could, for example, be used to prohibit a child's removal from the country where no residence order has been made and therefore no automatic restriction on removal applies or to prevent the child's removal from his home before the court has had time to decide what order, if any, should be made. A prohibited steps order may be made against anyone but can only prohibit "a step which could be taken by a parent in meeting his parental responsibility" for the child. It could not therefore be used, for example, to restrict publicity about a child since this is not within the scope of parental responsibility.

Specific issue orders

2.32. Specific issue orders may be made in conjunction with residence or contact orders or on their own. The aim, however, is not to give one parent or the other a general 'right' to make decisions about a particular aspect of the child's upbringing, for example his education or medical treatment, but rather to enable a particular dispute over such a matter to be resolved by the court, including the giving of detailed directions where necessary.

2.33. Although wardship will still be an available option in private disputes, the intention is that its use by individuals will be greatly reduced by the introduction of prohibited steps and specific issues orders. Local authority use of wardship has been severely restricted by section 100, which provides that the jurisdiction cannot be used for the purpose of placing a child in care, or in local authority accommodation, or under the supervision of a local authority (section 100(2) and paragraph 3.98 below). Local authorities will, like anyone else, be able to apply for specific issue and prohibited steps orders, provided that they first obtain the court's leave (see paragraph 2.43 below). This will enable them to resolve certain issues which at present can only be resolved by making the child a ward of court, such as whether or not he should have a particular operation. They may arise where a child is accommodated voluntarily by the authority, is felt to be in need of a particular course of treatment urgently and the parents cannot be contacted. If, in all the circumstances of the case, the decision is likely to cause controversy at some future date, the local authority should seek a section 8 specific issue order. Local authorities will not, however, be able to do this if the child is subject to a care order, as the only section 8 order which may be made in such cases is a residence order. Nor can they apply for a prohibited steps or specific issue order as a way of obtaining the care or supervision of a child, nor to obtain an order that the child be accommodated by them, nor can a prohibited steps or specific issue order confer any aspect of parental responsibility upon an authority (section 9(5)(b)).

2.34. Similarly, a prohibited steps or specific issue order may not be made "with a view to achieving a result which could be achieved by making a residence or contact order" (section 9(5)(a)). This is to avoid either of these orders being used to achieve much the same practical results as residence and contact orders but without the same legal effects.

THE MEANING OF 'FAMILY PROCEEDINGS'

2.35. The court may make a section 8 order with respect to a child in any family proceedings in which a question arises with respect to the welfare of that child (section 10(1)). 'Family proceedings' are defined by section 8(3) as any proceedings:

"(a) under the inherent jurisdiction of the High Court in relation to children; and

(b) under the enactments mentioned in subsection (4), but does not include proceedings on an application for leave under section 100(3)."

The enactments listed in section 8(4) are: Parts I, II and IV of the Children Act, the Matrimonial Causes Act 1973, the Domestic Violence and Matrimonial Proceedings Act 1976, the Adoption Act 1976, the Domestic Proceedings and Magistrates' Courts Act 1978, sections 1 and 9 of the Matrimonial Homes Act 1983 and Part III of the Matrimonial and Family Proceedings Act 1984.

2.36. Section 8 orders may therefore be made in most proceedings specifically relating to the care and upbringing of children, that is wardship proceedings, proceedings under the Act itself, including applications for care and supervision orders and adoption proceedings, but not emergency protection and child assessment proceedings under Part V of the Act or secure accommodation proceedings under section 25, which is in Part III. Orders may also be made in certain proceedings which are primarily concerned with disputes between adults but in which the interests of the children may be very important. These include divorce, nullity and judicial separation proceedings, maintenance proceedings in magistrates' courts, and domestic violence or ouster proceedings in both magistrates' and the higher courts.

APPLICATIONS FOR SECTION 8 ORDERS

2.37. Section 8 orders may be made either on application or of the court's own motion under section 10(1) in the course of family proceedings or, in the absence of any other proceedings, on a freestanding application under section 10(2). Section 10 also sets out the three basic categories of applicants for section 8 orders.

2.38. In the first category are people who may apply as of right for *any* section 8 order. These are (a) parents (including unmarried fathers) and guardians; and (b) any person in whose favour a residence order is in force with respect to the child (section 10(4)).

2.39. In the second category are people who may apply as of right for a residence or contact order. These are (a) any party to a marriage (whether or not subsisting) in relation to whom the child is a child of the family; (b) any person with whom the child has lived for a period of at least three years and (c) any person who; (i) where a residence order is in force with respect to the child has the consent of each of the persons in whose favour the order was made; (ii) where the child is in the care of a local authority has the consent of that authority; or (iii) in any other case has the consent of each of those (if any) who have parental responsibility for the child (section 10(5)).

2.40. Group (a) in this category consists primarily of step-parents. "Child of the family" is now defined, as in section 88(1) of the Domestic Proceedings and Magistrates' Courts Act 1978, as "(a) a child of both parties; or (b) any other child, not being a child who is placed with those parties as foster parents by a local authority or voluntary organisation, who has been treated by both those parties as a child of their family" (section 105(1)). Children formerly *privately* fostered may therefore be included.

2.41. Groups (b) and (c) in this category cover much the same people as those who could previously apply under the custodianship procedure (repealed by the Act), but with considerable simplification. People who have the consent of those whose rights will be affected if any order is made can apply whether or not the child is currently living with them. People who do not have the consent must have had the child living with them for a total of three years. The period of three years need not be continuous but must not have begun more than five years before, or ended more than three months before, the making of the application (section 10(10)). The three months will give them time to make an application if the child is removed against their wishes and so the previous complex provisions (in sections 41 and 42 of the Children Act 1975) prohibiting the removal of a child who had been with the applicants for three years have been repealed. The procedure has also been simplified, in that it is no longer necessary for the local authority to investigate and report to the court in every case. Instead, as in any case where a court is considering any question with respect to a child under the Act, the court is empowered to call for a welfare officer's report under section 7, either from a probation officer or from the local authority.

2.42. It is provided by section 10(6) that any person who does not otherwise fall into either of the first two categories is nevertheless entitled to apply for the variation or discharge of a section 8 order if either the order was made on his application or, in the case of a contact order, he is named in the order.

2.43. The third category covers anyone else with the leave of the court, who may apply for *any* section 8 order (although in the case of local authorities and their foster parents there are certain restrictions, which will be dealt with below). This enables anyone with a genuine interest in the child's welfare to apply for a section 8 order and should avoid the need to use wardship. The child himself can apply for leave, which may be granted if the court is satisfied that he has sufficient understanding to make the proposed application (section 10(8)). Where the applicant is not the child concerned, the court must have particular regard to a number of factors in deciding whether to grant leave. These are: the nature of the proposed application, any risk of the proposed application disrupting the child's life to such an extent that he would be harmed by it and, where the child is being looked after by a local authority, the authority's plans for the child's future and the wishes and feelings of the child's parents (section 10(9)).

2.44. Although under the previous law grandparents had the right to apply in certain circumstances for access under section 14 of the Domestic Proceedings and Magistrates' Courts Act 1978 and section 14A of the Guardianship of Minors Act 1971 (which are repealed by the 1989 Act) it is not intended that they be included in the category of persons entitled to apply for a section 8 order without leave. On the other hand, they are unlikely to have difficulty in obtaining leave to apply so that their position should on the whole be better than under the previous law, which did not allow freestanding applications by grandparents.

The position of local authority foster parents

2.45. Local authority foster parents are subject to the additional restriction that they cannot apply for leave to make an application for a section 8 order with respect to a child they have fostered at any time within the past six months, unless they also have the consent of the local authority (section 9(3)). This means that local authority foster parents fall into four categories:

(a) those with whom the child had lived for a total of at least three years during the previous five, who may apply as of right for a residence or contact order;

(b) those who have the consent of the people whose rights will be affected by the order, who may apply as of right for a residence or contact order. The people affected will either be all those with parental responsibility for the child, or if there is already a residence order, or if the child is the subject of a care order, the local authority concerned;

(c) relatives of the child, who will need leave to make any application if they do not fall within the first two rules, but do not need the additional consent of the local authority; and

(d) everyone else, who will need both the consent of the local authority and the leave of the court to make an application for any sort of section 8 order; this restriction is to prevent applications by foster parents at a stage when the local authority is still trying to assess what is best for the child in the long term and also so that parents will not be deterred from asking for their child to be accommodated with a local authority foster parent if the need arises.

The position of local authorities

2.46. The Act draws a clear distinction between children being provided with accommodation or other services by a local authority and children formally in the care of a local authority. Parental responsibility for a child may only be acquired by a local authority by means of a care order, which will only be granted if the criteria set out in section 31 are met. For this reason a local authority may not in any circumstances apply for or be granted a residence or contact order (section 9(2)). Furthermore, once a care order has been made in respect of a child, the court's private law powers should not be used to interfere with the local authority's exercise of its statutory parental responsibilities. It is therefore provided by section 9(1) that no court shall make any section 8 order, other than a residence order, with respect to a child in care. The restrictions in section 9(1) do *not*, however, apply where the child is being voluntarily accommodated by the local authority under Part III of the Act.

2.47. This means that if an individual is unhappy with the arrangements decided on by the local authority for contact with a child in care, he or she must apply to the court under section 34 of the Act. It also means that not only are individuals prevented from applying for prohibited steps or specific issue orders as a means of challenging the decisions of a local authority with respect to a child in its care, but the local authority itself cannot seek guidance from the court on matters concerning the child's upbringing by applying for one of these orders once the child is formally in its care. Instead, the local authority will have to apply for leave to invoke the High Court's inherent jurisdiction under section 100(3). The only section 8 order that may be made in respect of a child in care is a residence order which, under section 91(1), has the effect of discharging the care order.

2.48. However, a local authority will be able to apply for leave to make an application for a specific issue or prohibited steps order with respect to a child who is not in its care under a care order, whether or not the child is being provided with accommodation or other services under the Act. The court will have to consider the usual criteria for granting leave under section 10(9) (see paragraph 2.43 above) but if the action which the local authority wishes to take or prevent falls within the scope of parental responsibility (see paragraph 2.2 above), then a specific issue or prohibited steps order may be available and the local authority will not be able to invoke the inherent jurisdiction.

Older children

2.49. Sections 9(6) and 9(7) provide respectively that the court shall not make any section 8 order which is to have effect beyond a child's sixteenth birthday nor should an order be made once the child has reached the age of sixteen unless the court is satisfied that the circumstances of the case are exceptional. This confirms the previous practice of the courts in relation to custody and access orders that there is little point in making such an order against the wishes of a young person of this age. An example of exceptional circumstances might be where the child concerned is mentally handicapped. In such circumstances, an order may continue until the child is eighteen.

FAMILY ASSISTANCE ORDERS

2.50. Section 16 of the Act provides for a new type of order known as the family assistance order. It may be made in *any* family proceedings where the court has power to make an order under Part II with respect to any child, whether or not it actually makes such an order, and can only be made by the court acting of its own motion. The family assistance order must be distinguished from a supervision order under section 31. Together, these replace the courts' power to make a supervision order in private law proceedings (under section 44(1) of the Matrimonial Causes Act 1973, under section 2(2)(a) of the Guardianship Act 1973, under section 9 of the Domestic Proceedings and Magistrates' Courts Act 1978 and under section 26 of the Adoption Act 1976, all of which are repealed by Schedule 15, and in wardship proceedings under section 7(4) of the Family Law Reform Act 1969, which is repealed by section 100(1)). A supervision order is designed for the more serious cases, in which there is an element of child protection involved, and access to the local authority's facilities and services may be particularly important; the threshold criteria in section 31 must be proved, the supervisor will normally be the local authority, and there is power to impose additional requirements upon the child and upon the adults responsible for him. By contrast, a family assistance order aims simply to provide short-term help to a family, to overcome the problems and conflicts associated with their separation or divorce. Help may well be focused more on the adults than the child.

2.51. The order will require a probation officer to be made available, or a local authority to make an officer of the authority available, "to advise, assist and (where appropriate) befriend any person named in the order" (section 16(1)).

The persons who may be named in the order are:

(a) any parent or guardian of the child;

(b) any person with whom the child is living or in whose favour a contact order is in force with respect to the child;

(c) the child himself.

The order may also require any of the persons named in it to take specified steps with a view to enabling the officer concerned to be kept informed of the address of any person named in the order and to be allowed to visit any such person (section 16(4)).

2.52. A family assistance order can only be made if the court is satisfied that the circumstances of the case are exceptional (section 16(3)(a)). It should not therefore be made as a matter of routine. Furthermore, it will be particularly important in all orders for the court to make plain at the outset why family assistance is needed and what it is hoped to achieve by it. As the aim of the order is to provide voluntary assistance, it is also necessary for the court to obtain the consent of every person to be named in the order, except the child (section 16(3)(b)). Since it is intended as a short-term remedy only, no order can have effect for a period of more than six months (section 16(5)), although there is no restriction on making any further order.

2.53. When both a family assistance order and a section 8 order are in force at the same time with respect to a child, the officer concerned may refer to the court the question whether the section 8 order should be varied or discharged (section 16(6)). A family assistance order can only require a local authority to make an officer available with authority's consent or if the child concerned lives or will live within the authority's area (section 16(7)) and where an order requires a probation officer to be made available, he shall be selected in accordance with the arrangements made by the probation committee for the area in which the child lives or will live (section 16(8)).

THE COURT'S DUTY WHEN CONSIDERING WHETHER TO MAKE AN ORDER

2.54. The general principle set out in section 1(5) that the court should not make an order "unless it considers that doing so would be better for the child than making no order at all" applies whenever the court is considering whether to make one or more orders under the Act and therefore applies equally to private and public law proceedings.

2.55. The operation of this principle will be particularly noticeable in divorce and judicial separation proceedings since section 41 of the Matrimonial Causes Act 1973 no longer requires the court to make a declaration that the arrangements proposed for the children are "satisfactory" or "the best that can be devised in the circumstances" before granting a decree. The parties still have to provide information to the court about the proposed arrangements but the court is no longer required in every case to approve those arrangements. Instead, the duty of the court is limited to considering whether it should exercise any of its powers under the Act. It may feel, for example, that an investigation and report by a welfare officer is necessary or, in a disputed case, that it should make a residence or contact order. Postponement of the decree absolute may only be ordered where the court needs time to give further consideration to the case and there are exceptional circumstances which make it desirable in the interests of the child (schedule 12, paragraph 31).

2.56. There are several situations where the court is likely to consider it better for the child to make an order than not. If the court has had to resolve a dispute between the parents, it is likely to be better for the child to make an order about it. Even if there is no dispute, the child's need for stability and security may be better served by making an order. There may also be specific legal advantages in doing so. One example is where abduction of the child is a possibility, since a court order is necessary for enforcement proceedings in other parts of the

United Kingdom under the Family Law Act 1986, and under the European Convention and under the Hague Convention an order will be necessary if the aggrieved party is, for example, an unmarried father or a relative who would not otherwise have 'rights of custody'. An advantage of having a residence order is that the child may be taken out of the country for periods of less than a month without the permission of other persons with parental authority or the court, whereas without an order this could amount to an offence under the Child Abduction Act 1984. Also if a person has a sole residence order in his favour and appoints a temporary guardian for the child, the appointment will take effect immediately on that person's death, even where there is a surviving parent. Depending on the circumstances of the case, the court might therefore be persuaded that an order would be in the child's interest.

2.57. The welfare principle, set out in section 1(1) of the Act, requires that whenever a court determines any question with respect to (a) the upbringing of a child; or (b) the administration of a child's property or the application of any income arising from it, the child's welfare shall be the court's paramount consideration. Not all proceedings affecting children's upbringing or property are governed by the welfare principle. For example, it is expressly excluded by section 105(1) from applications for maintenance for a child and section 6 of the Adoption Act 1976 provides that the child's welfare shall be the "first" consideration, as it is in proceedings relating to property and financial issues on divorce by section 25(1) of the Matrimonial Causes Act 1973. On an application for an order under section 1 of the Matrimonial Homes Act 1983 the welfare of the child is neither first nor paramount. It is merely one of the factors to which the court must have regard. It does, however, apply whenever a court is considering whether to make a section 8 order, regardless of the type of proceedings in which the issue arises. The child's welfare would, therefore, be paramount if the court were considering making a section 8 order in, for example, adoption proceedings (see also paragraph 2.64 below).

2.58. In determining what is in the child's best interests, the court is required, in all contested applications for section 8 orders, or for variation or discharge of such orders (as it is in all proceedings for orders under Part IV, or for their variation or discharge, whether contested or uncontested) to have regard to the checklist of relevant factors set out in section 1(3).

2.59. It should be noted, however, that the checklist does not apply in all 'family proceedings', but only in contested private proceedings under Part II and any proceedings under Part IV of the Act. Thus, although adoption proceedings are 'family proceedings', and therefore any section 8 order *may* be made, the court is not required to have regard to the checklist and therefore is under no duty to consider what alternatives may be available.

2.60. Section 1(2) requires the court "in any proceedings in which any question with regard to the upbringing of a child arises" to "have regard to the general principle that any delay in determining the question is likely to prejudice the welfare of the child". This principle thus applies equally to private proceedings, including those brought other than under the Children Act, and public proceedings.

THE RELATIONSHIP BETWEEN PRIVATE LAW ORDERS AND PUBLIC LAW PROCEEDINGS

2.61. Because the court is required to have regard to the statutory checklist whenever it is considering whether to make, vary or discharge an order under Part IV of the Act, it must consider whether a different order from the one applied for might be more appropriate and since care and supervision proceedings come within the definition of 'family proceedings' in section 8(3), the court has the power to make any section 8 order as an alternative. Thus, for example, the court might decide, on an application for a care order, that the child's interests would be better served by making a residence order in favour of, say, a relative. The threshold criteria under section 31(2) do not then have to be met. It will therefore be important for those considering care proceedings to consider the alternative possibilities, and in particular the extent to which the child's needs might be met within the extended family, with an appropriate combination of section 8 orders and the provision of local authority services under Part III of the Act. The range of section 8 orders is extremely flexible, allowing the court to provide the child with very similar protection to that which is available in wardship.

2.62. The court may also make a section 8 order as an interim measure when a care application is pending. Section 11(3) provides that the court may make a section 8 order at any time during the course of the proceedings in question even though it is not in a position to dispose finally of those proceedings and section 11(7) enables a section 8 order to be made for a specified period. The court could therefore, for example, make a residence order in favour of another family member, or a foster parent, until the date of the hearing and regulate the child's contact with his parents by means of a contact order or prevent it altogether by means of a prohibited steps order. It should be noted however, that if, pending an application for a care of supervision order the court decides to make a residence order with respect to the child, it must also make an interim supervision order "unless satisfied that his welfare will be satisfactorily safeguarded without an interim order being made" (section 38(3)).

2.63. Although under section 39 application may be made for discharge of a care order, or discharge or variation of a supervision order, by any person who has parental responsibility for the child, or the child himself or the local authority/supervisor concerned, those without parental responsibility, such as unmarried fathers and other relatives of the child, have no right to make such an application. They may, however, apply for a residence order which, if granted, would have the effect of discharging any existing care order by virtue of section 91(1). Since a residence order not only provides for the child to live with the person in whose favour it is made but also gives parental responsibility to that person while the order is in force (or, in the case of an unmarried father, he will acquire it by virtue of a separate order under section 4), the continuation of a care order would be inconsistent with the making of a residence order. Equally, the making of a care order with respect to a child who is the subject of a section 8 order will discharge that order (section 91(2)) and the making of a care order with respect to a child who is a ward of court will bring the wardship to an end (section 91(4)).

SECTION 8 ORDERS IN ADOPTION PROCEEDINGS

2.64. Adoption proceedings are 'family proceedings' and it is therefore open to the court to make any section 8 order either as an alternative or in addition to an adoption order. Thus the court would be able to make a residence order instead of an adoption order in favour of step-parent, relative or foster parent, whenever this would be better for the child. The previous restrictions on making alternative orders (contained in section 37 of the Children Act 1975) no longer apply, but neither is there any statutory duty to consider doing so (as existed in step-parent applications by virtue of sections 14(3) and 15(4) of the Adoption Act 1976 and section 37 of the Children Act 1975). It therefore remains to be seen whether the courts will feel that it is their duty to consider whether, for example, a residence order would be more appropriate than an adoption order in all or any such cases.

2.65. It is now open to third parties to apply, or at least to seek leave to apply, for section 8 orders in adoption proceedings. Thus, for example, grandparents may wish to apply for a contact order on an adoption application. Technically, an adoption order extinguishes any existing order under the Children Act (section 12(3)(a) of the Adoption Act 1976) but the court would have power to make a section 8 order of its own motion once the adoption order had been made. The same applies after an order freeing the child for adoption. Hitherto, however, the courts have been reluctant to make access a condition of an adoption order without the agreement of the adoptive parents.

2.66. The Children Act has created a new statutory code governing financial provision for children, which is contained in section 15 and Schedule 1. This consists primarily of the re-enactment, with consequential amendments and minor modifications, of the relevant provisions of the Guardianship of Minors Act 1971, the Guardianship Act 1973, the Children Act 1975 and the Family Law Reform Act 1987. The aim is to simplify and rationalise the law. All applications concerning financial relief for a child only, and not for an adult as well, will now have to be made under the 1989 Act and qualify as 'family proceedings' as defined in section 8(3), so that the court is also able to make any section 8 order in those proceedings. The courts will still have power, however, to make orders for financial provision for children in matrimonial proceedings under the Matrimonial Causes Act 1973 and the Domestic Proceedings and Magistrates' Courts Act 1978. Applications under the schedule may be made by a parent or guardian or by any person in whose favour a residence order is in force with respect to the child (schedule 1, paragraph 1(1)).

CHAPTER 3 CARE AND SUPERVISION ORDERS

3.1. The new legal scheme for civil care and supervision proceedings is founded on a number of principles. The first is that compulsory intervention in the care and upbringing of a child will be possible only by court order following proceedings under the new statutory scheme, in which the child, his parents and others who are connected with the child will be able to participate fully. The proceedings should establish what action, if any, is in the child's interests, and the procedure should be as fair as possible to all concerned. The term 'care' is used in the Act in relation to a child subject to a care order and not to a child accommodated by a local authority under voluntary arrangements. Guidance on the implications of the Children Act for juvenile offending (see Chapter 6) covers criminal care and supervision orders.

3.2. Second, a care or supervision order will be sought only when there appears to be no better way of safeguarding and promoting the welfare of the child suffering, or likely to suffer, significant harm. The local authority has a general duty to promote the upbringing of children in need by their families so far as this is consistent with its duty to promote children's welfare and to avoid the need for proceedings where possible; it should have regard to the court's presumption against making an order in section 1(5) while at the same time giving paramount consideration to the child's welfare. This means that voluntary arrangements through the provision of services to the child and his family should always be fully explored. Where a care or supervision order is the appropriate remedy because control of the child's circumstances is necessary to promote his welfare, applications in such proceedings should be part of a carefully planned process. The new scheme imposes strict conditions which have to be met but does not place unnecessary obstacles in the way of action that is necessary to protect the child. It also increases opportunities to apply for discharge and variation of care orders and supervision orders.

3.3. Third, there will be common grounds for making care or supervision orders irrespective of the route by which cases proceed. These will need to address present or prospective harm to the child and how this is occurring or may occur. Factors such as failure to receive suitable education and committing an offence will no longer be grounds in themselves for making a care or supervision order except in so far as they contribute to the harm done and may be attributable to the parenting, or lack of proper parenting.

3.4. Fourth, there will be greater emphasis on representing the views, feelings and needs of the child in these proceedings. Guardians *ad litem* must now be appointed in most kinds of public law proceedings where statutory intervention is sought under the Act unless the court is satisfied that this is not necessary in order to safeguard the child's interests. Where a guardian *ad litem* is to be appointed the appointment should be made as soon as the application is received by the court or as appropriate, and should help the court prevent unnecessary delay in dealing with the case. Where an application for a care or supervision order follows on from the making of an emergency protection order or child assessment order a guardian *ad litem* will usually already have been appointed.

3.5. Fifth, when a care order is in force the local authority and parents share parental responsibility for the child subject to the authority's power to limit the exercise of such responsibility by the parents in order to safeguard the child's welfare, and to some specific limitations on the authority. The Act also establishes a presumption of reasonable parental contact with children in care, subject to court orders and limited local authority action in emergencies.

APPLICATIONS FOR CARE AND SUPERVISION ORDERS (SECTIONS 31 AND 32)

Order-making powers

3.6. The Children Act establishes that no child may be placed in the care of a local authority or put under the supervision of a local authority or probation officer in civil proceedings except by action under the statutory scheme in sections 31 et seq. Various routes into care or supervision under the Children and Young Persons Act 1969 and other legislation have been abolished. So has the use of the High Court's inherent jurisdiction to put a child into local authority care (Section 100(2)(a)), and the power of a court in criminal proceedings to make a care order (Section 90(1) and (2)). Supervision orders may still be made in juvenile criminal proceedings under the Children and Young Persons Act 1969, as amended by Schedule 12 to the Children Act, but these differ in important respects from supervision orders made under the new civil scheme (see paragraph 6.16 below).

3.7. Care and supervision proceedings, and indeed all proceedings under Part IV, are 'family proceedings' (section 8(3)), and for the first time may be heard in the High Court and county courts as well as in the new family proceedings courts of the magistrates' courts (section 92(7)). The court hearing an application for a care order or supervision order may make any section 8 order as an alternative to a care order or supervision order, or in combination with a supervision order, on application or on its own initiative. A court in any other family proceedings may also make a care or supervision order if the requirements of section 31 are met, either on an application following a direction to the local authority under section 37 or on an application by a local authority or authorised person in the proceedings. This means a local authority or authorised person may apply for a care or supervision order in any proceedings under:

(a) the inherent jurisdiction of the High Court in relation to children;

(b) Parts I,II and IV of the Children Act 1989;

(c) the Matrimonial Causes Act 1973;

(d) the Domestic Violence and Matrimonial Proceedings Act 1976;

(e) the Adoption Act 1976;

(f) the Domestic Proceedings and Magistrates' Courts Act 1978;

(g) sections 1 and 9 of the Matrimonial Homes Act 1983;

(h) part III of the Matrimonial and Family Proceedings Act 1984.

3.8. In practice, the residence order is likely to be the most common of the section 8 alternatives to care and supervision orders albeit that a local authority cannot apply for a residence order on behalf of itself or a third party. Specific issue orders and prohibited steps orders cannot be used to achieve what may be achieved by the other section 8 orders, namely where the child should live and who should have contact with him (section 9(5)), but may be used by local authorities in respect of a child *not* in their care, and others, to resolve other specially difficult matters which might previously have been referred to the wardship court. Contact with children in care is provided for specifically in section 34.

Matters to be considered when deciding whether to apply for a care order or supervision order

3.9. Only a local authority or authorised person (as defined in section 31(9)) may apply for a care or supervision order. At present only the NSPCC is authorised. It is no longer possible for local education authorities and the police to initiate these proceedings. The Act also repeals section 3 of the Children and

Young Persons Act 1963, which allowed a parent or guardian to apply for an order directing a local authority to bring a child before a juvenile court. The rationale for these changes is that it is the local authority alone which has statutory responsibility for investigating where a child is thought to be suffering harm, for promoting the upbringing of children in need by their families and, indeed, for reducing the need to bring care proceedings; and which would be responsible for looking after the child or for supervising him (unless, and in cases not usually involving child protection, a probation officer is appointed instead) if an order were made.

3.10. This limitation places a special responsibility on the local authority. The authority cannot expect to be sole repository of knowledge and wisdom about particular cases. Full inter-agency co-operation including sharing information and participating in decision-making is essential whenever a possible care or supervision case is identified. The local authority should lead by example and be prepared to make full use of the new provisions on co-operation between agencies in sections 47 (investigations) and 27 (exercise of Part III functions). A multi-disciplinary, multi-agency case conference should always be held, based on the principles and arrangements set out in 'Working Together' and local guidelines on joint planning and co-operation, and it should seek to recommend an agreed course of action. Parents, the child (if of sufficient age and understanding) and others with a legitimate interest in the child's future should be involved wherever possible. Involvement will mean more than just attendance; families should be able to participate in the decision-making process and they will need to be kept informed of decisions as they are made, the reasoning behind those decisions and their likely consequences. No decision to initiate proceedings should be taken without clear evidence that provision of services for the child and his family (which may include an accommodation placement voluntarily arranged under section 20) has failed or would be likely to fail to meet the child's needs adequately (see paragraphs 3.19 and 3.20 on significant harm) and that there is no suitable person prepared to apply to take over care of the child under a residence order.

3.11. Local authorities should in particular be guided by the founding principle set out in paragraph 3.2 in considering these matters. Having identified the child's needs, they should consider in each case whether any of the services which the authority provides, or could provide, under Part III and Schedule 2 (or which might be available from voluntary organisations or others) would be likely to improve the situation sufficiently (see Volume 2). Where parents are struggling to care for the child, home-help, day care, parenting advice, voluntary befriending and other support of this kind, coupled with close monitoring of the child's welfare by a health visitor and social worker, or a temporary placement for the child in local authority accommodation under voluntary arrangements, may retrieve the situation. What will use of compulsory powers add in safeguarding the child and is the gain sufficient to justify use of compulsion and the trauma that may result? Options should always be discussed with the parents or others having parental responsibility for the child, and with the child himself (unless very young) in language appropriate to his understanding. Care or supervision proceedings should not be presented as a threat, but the parents should always understand where, in the absence of adequate parenting and co-operation, exercise of the authority's responsibilities and duties will lead.

3.12. Before proceeding with an application, the local authority social services department should always seek legal advice (preferably within the context of the multi-disciplinary, multi-agency case conference) on:

(a) whether, in the circumstances of the case and having regard to the section 1(3) checklist, the court is likely to be satisfied first that the section 31(2) criteria are satisfied and then that an order should be made under the section 1(5) test;

(b) the implications of another party to the proceedings opposing the application and applying for a section 8 order instead;

(c) whether the application falls within criteria of transfer of cases to a higher court and whether representations about this should be made;

(d) whether the court should be asked for an interim care or supervision order, the desired length of the initial interim order and what directions should be sought;

(e) the matters to be provided for in the authority's advance statement of case including copies of witness statements that can be made available and a broad outline of the authority's plans for the child;

(f) notification and other procedural requirements and matters likely to be considered at a directions appointment;

(g) whether the court is likely to consider that in all the circumstances of the case a guardian *ad litem* does not need to be appointed;

(h) whether use of a residence order linked with a supervision order would be an appropriate alternative to a care order.

3.13. An authorised person proposing to apply for a care or supervision order must first consult the local authority if it is reasonably practicable for him to do so (section 31(6)). What is 'reasonably practicable' should be considered in the context of 'Working Together' and local guidelines on inter-agency relationships, responsibility and accountability for effective case management. He should establish from the authority whether the child is the subject of any application or order specified in section 31(7) i.e. an application for a care order or supervision order which has not been disposed of; a care order or supervision order (including a deemed care or supervision order under the Act's transitional provisions); a supervision order in juvenile criminal proceedings under section 7(7)(b) of the Children and Young Persons Act 1969; or a supervision or residential requirement imposed by a children's hearing under section 44(1) of the Social Work (Scotland) Act 1968.

3.14. As a matter of good practice, authorised persons should always keep the local authority informed of their concerns about children in the authority's area, including any accommodated by the authority, and share their information and thinking as matters develop and the need for intervention becomes apparent. They should seek to agree a course of action – for example, that the authorised person should proceed with his application or should modify it, that the authority take it over instead, or that it be postponed pending further enquiries or other action. The authority should look carefully into the authorised person's case, consulting other agencies and following the guidelines in paragraph 3.11. It will be necessary to balance speed and thoroughness in making these enquiries in urgent cases; having the matter out in court should only be necessary if there is a genuine difference of opinion between the authority and the authorised person.

Conditions for a care or supervision order

3.15. The child must be under age seventeen (or under 16 if married, for example where a child was married outside the UK). The court may not consider an application from an authorised person if, at the time the application is made, the child was subject to an application or order specified in section 31(7). These points should be checked by the authority or other applicant as part of the process of deciding whether to apply. The court is likely to look particularly keenly at a case for making an order for a young person who is approaching his seventeenth birthday (or sixteenth, if married). The order ceases to have effect at age eighteen unless brought to an end earlier (section 91); unlike the position in previous legislation, it is no longer possible to extend the period of care to age 19 in certain circumstances.

3.16. The court may not make an order unless satisfied that (section 31(2)):

(a) the child concerned is suffering significant harm, or is likely to suffer significant harm; and

(b) the harm or likelihood of harm is attributable to

   (i) the care given to the child, or likely to be given to him if the order were not made, not being what it would be reasonable to expect a parent to give him; or

   (ii) the child is beyond parental control.

But even if these conditions are met the court is not obliged to make the order. It must go on to apply the child-centred principles of section 1 of the Act, namely that the welfare of the child is the paramount consideration, the checklist of factors to be considered, and the presumption of no order. Thus where the prognosis for change is reasonable and parents show a willingness to co-operate with voluntary arrangements, an application for a care or supervision order is unlikely to succeed. The court must also consider the wide range of powers available to it to make other orders and to give directions.

3.17. The threshold criteria in section 31(2) replace the various conditions for care and supervision orders in previous legislation such as committing an offence or non-attendance at school. These orders can now only be made under these provisions. The grounds in previous legislation were largely confined to an examination of present and past deficits in the development or well-being of the child. Where the likelihood of future harm was at issue, the local authority sometimes thought it necessary to apply to the High Court for wardship. The new grounds are concerned with present or future harm: care or supervision should not be sought unless the child is currently suffering significant harm or would be likely to suffer significant harm if the order were not made. Current or anticipated harm may have its origins in past harm, of course, but there would have to be evidence of significant harm continuing or being likely to continue. With this change of emphasis, the wardship route to care and supervision is not required and is no longer available. Local authorities will still, however, in exceptional circumstances and with the leave of the court be able to invoke the High Court's inherent jurisdiction to resolve specific issues concerning a child in its care (section 100(2)) (see paragraphs 3.98 – 3.103 below).

3.18. Looking at the threshold criteria in more detail, there are two limbs and both have to be satisfied. The first focuses on present or anticipated harm. The second is that the harm, or likelihood of harm, is attributable to the parenting of the child or to the child's being beyond parental control.

3.19. 'Harm' is defined in section 31(9) as ill-treatment or the impairment of health or development. It is important to note that these are alternatives. Only one of these conditions needs to be satisfied but the proceedings may refer to all three. Ill-treatment is defined, again in section 31(9), as including sexual abuse and forms of ill-treatment that are not physical, as for example emotional abuse. It includes physical abuse by implication. Ill-treatment is sufficient proof of harm in itself and it is not necessary to show that impairment of health or development has followed, or is likely to follow (although that might be relevant to later stages of the test). Thus a child who is injured but has made a complete recovery, could be demonstrated to have suffered harm for the purposes of the proceedings. It is additionally necessary to show that the ill-treatment is significant, which given its dictionary definition means considerable, noteworthy or important. The 'significance' could exist in the seriousness of the harm or in the implication of it. This will be a finding of fact for the court.

3.20. In most cases impairment of health or development is likely to provide the basis of harm. Health is defined in section 31(9) as physical or mental health; development as physical, intellectual, emotional, social or behavioural development, so that a child that is failing to control his anti-social behaviour would, for example, be included. As with ill-treatment, it is necessary to show that the impairment in any or all aspects of the child's health or development is significant where the significance is demonstrated by what could be reasonably expected of a similar child. The meaning of 'similar' in this context will require judicial interpretation, but may need to take account of environmental, social and cultural characteristics of the child. The need to use a standard appropriate for the child in question arises because some children have characteristics or handicaps which mean that they cannot be expected to be as healthy or well-developed as others. Equally, if the child needs special care or attention (because, for example, he is unusually difficult to control) then this is to be expected for him. The standard should only be that which it is reasonable to expect for the particular child, rather than the best that could possibly be achieved; applying a 'best' standard could open up the risk that a child might be removed from home simply because some other arrangement could cater better for his needs than care by his parents.

3.21. Having set an acceptable standard of upbringing for the child, it is necessary to show some significant deficit in that standard. Minor shortcomings in health care or minor deficits in physical, psychological or social development should not require compulsory intervention unless cumulatively they are having, or are likely to have, serious and lasting effects upon the child. Early intervention is always preferable but remedial action under Part III of the Act or by the health authority is likely to be more appropriate. The court is required to decide whether the harm is significant where this is a matter of health and development by comparing the health and development of the child concerned with that of a hypothetical similar child. Drawing on advice as necessary, for example from the guardian *ad litem's* report or other expert advice, the court will have to establish what standard of health and development it would be reasonable to expect for a child with similar attributes, assess the shortfall in the health and development of the child in question against that standard, and decide whether the difference represents significant harm.

3.22. The 'likely to suffer significant harm' provision in the first limb replaces more restricted conditions in previous legislation. There is a complementary provision – "the care . . . likely to be given to the child if the order were not made . . . " – in the second limb (see paragraph 3.23). These provisions allow proceedings to be considered where, for example, the child had suffered significant harm at some time in the past and is likely to do so again because of some recurring circumstance, as for example where physical abuse of a child is associated with bouts of parental depression; or where a newly-born baby, because of the family history, would be at risk if taken home; or where the welfare of a child who was being looked after by the local authority under voluntary accommodation arrangements (section 20) would be at risk if the parents went ahead with plans to return him to an unsuitable home environment. At the same time the conditions are intended to place a sufficiently difficult burden of proof upon the applicant as to prevent unwarranted intervention in cases where the child is not genuinely at risk.

3.23. The second limb requires the court to be satisfied that "the harm, or likelihood of harm, is attributable to the care given or likely to be given, to the child not being what it would be reasonable for a parent to give to the child". Harm caused solely by a third party is therefore excluded (unless the parent has failed to prevent it) and will require other forms of intervention to safeguard the child. The care given to the child has to be compared not with what it would be reasonable to expect *the* parent to give to the child but with what it would be reasonable to expect *a* parent to give him. It follows from 'reasonable' in the text that the hypothetical parent would be a reasonable parent. The actual parents may be doing their best but are not able to meet the child's particular needs and are unwilling or incapable of making use of appropriate services. The standard of care which it would be reasonable to expect them to give may be very low. The court must compare the care being given to the child in question with what it would be reasonable to expect a reasonable parent to give him, having regard to his needs. If a child has particular difficulties relating to any aspect of his health or development this could require a higher standard of care than for the average child. The court will almost certainly expect to see professional evidence on the standard of care which could reasonably be expected of reasonable parents with support from community-wide services as appropriate where the child's needs are complex or demanding, or the lack of reasonable care is not immediately obvious. 'Care' is not defined but in the context of section 31 must mean providing for the child's health and total development (physical, intellectual, emotional, social and behavioural) and not just having physical charge of him.

3.24. The 'likely' element in section 31(2)(b)(i) complements that in the first limb (paragraph 3.22). It provides for cases where the child's standard of care is deteriorating or he is not at the time of the application being cared for by the parents but there would be reason for concern about his welfare if they started to look after him.

3.25. The alternative causal condition in the second limb is that the child is beyond parental control. This was provided for in previous legislation, but was not linked with harm to the child. It provides for cases where, whatever the standard of care available to the child, he is not benefiting from it because of lack of parental control. It is immaterial whether this is the fault of the parents or the child. Such behaviour frequently stems from distorted or stressed relationships between parent and child.

Initial hearings: court requirements and party status

3.26. Rules of court require the local authority or authorised person applying for a care or supervision order to serve a copy of the application on all the parties to the proceedings. The child and any person with parental responsibility for the child will automatically be given party status. The court may also direct that others be joined to the proceedings.

3.27. Previous legislation provided specifically for the grandparents of the child to be able to apply for party status in certain circumstances. They are not specifically mentioned now but they, and indeed any relative, will be able to apply for party status if they fall within any of the categories described above.

3.28. A separate application must be made for each child on the prescribed form. These have been designed so as to encourage the preparation of documentary evidence and early advance disclosure of relevant evidence to the court and other parties. In particular the applicant for a care or supervision order will be required to submit details of plans for the future care of the child and any requests for directions, including restrictions on contact. The level of details given will be determined to some extent by the stage reached in the investigation of the child's circumstances. Any plan should be able to address the checklist of factors identified in section 1(3) of the Act and will need to be more than embryonic given the presumption of no order in section 1(5).

3.29. On receipt of the application, the clerk of the court will consider whether the proceedings should be transferred to a higher court according to the criteria set out in the Allocation and Transfer Rules and whether a directions appointment should be held in advance of the first hearing. At a directions appointment, which may be held at any time during the course of the proceedings, directions may be issued on any of the following matters:

(a) timetable for the proceedings and directions to ensure the timetable is adhered to (this has to be done at some point in the proceedings, and the directions appointment is often the most convenient);

(b) the identity of the parties to the proceedings;

(c) the submission of evidence including experts' reports;

(d) the appointment of a guardian *ad litem* or solicitor;

(e) the date for a subsequent directions appointment, if any, or first hearing;

(f) the attendance of the child concerned;

(g) any other matters considered relevant.

3.30. Usually the court will not be able to decide the application for a care order or supervision order at the first hearing. The applicant should be ready to tell the court at the directions appointment:

(a) whether he is applying for an interim order and, if so, any directions under section 38(6);

(b) what plans the authority have made for safeguarding and promoting the child's welfare while the interim order is in force and, where an interim care order is sought, what type of placement is envisaged (see Volumes 3 and 4);

(c) in the case of an interim order, what proposals the authority have for allowing the child reasonable contact with his parents and others under section 34.

Timetable requirements (section 32)

3.31. It must be expected that the court hearing an application for a care or supervision order will normally need to adjourn the proceedings to a further hearing or hearings because it is not in a position to decide the application, even when it is not contested. The guardian *ad litem* will usually need time to make enquiries, establish the child's and others' views, investigate the applicant's plans and prepare a report and recommendations for the court. Other parties will need to prepare their case, instruct a solicitor where appropriate, obtain witness statements etc. The Act and rules of court allow for these requirements but make specific provisions designed to ensure that applications are dealt with as soon as possible. These start with the principle in section 1(2) that any delay in determining a question about the upbringing of a child is likely to prejudice his welfare.

3.32. Research has identified a number of factors giving rise to adjournments which should be alleviated by the new arrangements for organising court business (see also rules of court) – for example, difficulties in obtaining court dates, arranging representation of the child, ensuring the presence of all participants and their representatives and appointing a guardian *ad litem*. It may be thought that widening access to party status and extending the role of guardians *ad litem* will make care and supervision proceedings more protracted but this should be offset by the new requirements on advance disclosure of case and witness statements by all parties, and the emphasis on agreeing facts at the directions appointment. In addition, the court is required by section 32(1) to draw up a timetable with a view to disposing of the application without delay, and to give such directions as it considers appropriate for seeing that the timetable is adhered to. There is a corresponding section 11(1) and rules for proceedings where a section 8 order is being considered.

3.33. Keeping to a minimum the number of adjournments and the length of intervals between hearings is a major objective of the Act. The court will be expected to recognise the urgency of care and supervision proceedings and organise its domestic business accordingly, to examine possible delays at preliminary hearings, avoid slack in directions on timetabling, and with assistance from the guardian *ad litem* monitor compliance with directions and the progress of the case. Rules of court require guardians *ad litem* to assist and advise the court as to the timing of all or any part of the proceedings. The timetable should encourage expeditious handling of matters before the court whilst not discouraging sensible negotiations between the parties. The local authority should ensure that all staff concerned with a case before the court, including local authority legal staff and staff of other authorities and agencies who may be involved, are made aware of court directions on timetabling and do whatever is necessary to ensure compliance with those directions. The applicant for the order should regard it as part of his responsibilities to help both the court clerk and the guardian *ad litem* identify and deal with difficulties likely to cause delay.

3.34. The court may make an interim care order or interim supervision order in the circumstances described in paragraph 3.36. Where it does so the court can be expected to match the duration of the interim order to the adjournment period, having regard to the limits on length of interim orders in section 38.

3.35. The Act gives the court new powers to make an interim supervision order instead of an interim care order, which may be linked to a short-term residence order. The Act also extends rights to challenge an interim order by appeal or application for discharge. There are two main objectives – to enable the child to be suitably protected while proceedings are progressing where this is required, and to see that interim measures operate only for as long as is necessary. The court will be influenced by timetable considerations in deciding the duration of interim orders.

3.36. The court may make an interim care order or interim supervision order when it adjourns proceedings hearing an application for a full care or supervision order or directs the local authority to investigate a child's circumstances under section 37(1). New grounds have been introduced. The court has to be satisfied, whether the making of an interim order is contested or not, that there are *reasonable grounds for believing* that the child's circumstances fulfil the criteria for a full care or supervision order in section 31(2).

3.37. This test is not the same as for a full order which requires proof that the child is suffering or likely to suffer significant harm. It would not be realistic to require proof of the condition at the interim stage when the guardian *ad litem's* final report will probably not have been received and all evidence heard. The child's version of events may form an integral part of 'reasonable grounds for believing' as could, for example, medical evidence that certain symptoms were consistent with abuse. After further assessment this may be rejected at the full hearing. Court findings of fact leading to the making of interim orders should therefore not be binding on the court at the final hearing, and should not be regarded as prejudicial to any of the parties to the proceedings. As when making full orders, the court must also have regard to the child welfare principles and checklist in section 1(1)-(3), and to the presumption against making an order in section 1(5).

3.38. Interim care and supervision orders are similar in effect to full care and supervision orders except in two particulars; the court determines the duration of the interim order and may give directions to the local authority as to the medical or psychiatric examination of the child or other assessment (see paragraphs 3.52 and 3.65 – 3.74 below). These orders represent substantial, if temporary, intervention in the care and upbringing of the child, and should not be regarded as routine parts of an application for a full care or supervision order. The lesser interim supervision order – not previously available at this stage – may be sufficient; certain improvements have been made to the order which should make this a more effective means of achieving a degree of control short of acquisition of parental responsibility and the power to remove the child from home, both of which are conferred on the holder of an interim care order. It is useful for attaining a particular objective, for example that a very young child attends his local health centre for routine health and developmental check-ups.

3.39. An interim care order or interim supervision order will usually be the only way that protection can continue to be afforded to a child after expiry of an emergency protection order or a period of police protection, if such protection is required while enquiries are continuing. In cases where there were, and continue to be, indications that emergency action is warranted, safeguarding and protecting the child's welfare should be the first consideration. The authority should also consider carefully, if an interim care order is made, whether the child could be allowed to live with his family under the new requirements.

3.40. The new criteria for interim orders are intended to prevent 'rubber-stamping' of unopposed applications. The consequences of interim care are potentially so serious for the child and those with parental responsibility for him that such a step should always be fully examined by the court. The parents and others concerned should never be encouraged to consent to an interim order just to avoid the trauma of a court hearing. The new and less adversarial procedures for court hearings, the role of the directions appointment and advance disclosure, are intended to remove as much trauma as possible without loss of effectiveness. Nor will parental agreement be sufficient to satisfy the presumption of no order in section 1(5).

3.41. The court is able to make a section 8 order as an interim measure, but if it makes a residence order it must also make an interim supervision order unless satisfied that the child's welfare will be satisfactorily safeguarded without one (sections 11(3) and 38(3)). A residence order made in these or any other circumstances gives the person with whom the child would live parental responsibility for him while the order is in force. It may contain directions about how it is to be carried into effect, impose conditions which must be complied with, and be made to have effect for a specified period – which could be until the original care or supervision application is decided (section 11(7)). Questions of contact between the child and the parents or other persons, the child's education and other matters to do with his welfare during this period, could be dealt under these powers or by way of other section 8 orders (contact orders, specific issues orders and prohibited steps orders).

3.42. Where a suitable relative or other person connected with the child is prepared to look after him and is likely to be able to meet his needs at least for a trial period, the residence order – supported where necessary by an interim supervision order – offers an attractive alternative to the interim care order. The local authority should always weigh carefully the pros and cons of such an arrangement. While there might be some danger in an arrangement which did not give control of the placement to the local authority, a temporary residence order might obviate the need for a full care order later if the interim arrangement proved an effective way of promoting the child's welfare. The authority should ensure that support services provided under Part III are made available to help the person caring for the child under a short-term residence order to meet the child's needs while the order is in force.

3.43. The court has specific power to give directions on medical or psychiatric examination or other assessment of the child when it makes an interim care or interim supervision order (section 38(6)-see paragraphs 3.47 – 3.51 below). However, care proceedings should not be used simply to obtain an examination or assessment of the child. If the applicant's main concern at this stage is to secure such an examination or assessment and the parents cannot be persuaded to co-operate on a voluntary basis, a child assessment order should be sufficient. If the authority believes an interim order is likely to be necessary, even though the child does not need to be removed, an interim supervision order is to be preferred. Medical and other assessment directions may be necessary where a child assessment order reveals only a partial picture of harm or failure to thrive, the authority's concerns are not dispelled and further investigation is called for. Other directions provided for in Parts I and II of schedule 3 to the Act relating to supervision orders would be at the supervisor's discretion.

Duration of interim orders

3.44. In previous legislation the court could make interim orders for any period up to 28 days. The Act modifies the time limit to allow the court to make an initial interim order for up to 8 weeks. This should help avoid the unproductive return to court after four weeks, before the parties were ready to proceed, which was common before. An eight week duration should not, however, come to be regarded as standard practice. The court will decide the length of each and any subsequent order having regard to the presumption against delay and its timetabling directions including the date determined for the next hearing, and the time limits set in section 38(4). Before making a further interim order the court must satisfy itself that the criteria in sections 38(2) and 1(5) are still satisfied – not by going over the evidence again but by considering any change in the circumstances, any new evidence that may have come to light and any other relevant matter that may cast doubt on the benefit of a new order.

3.45. There are new time limits for all interim orders, although any party may bring the matter back to the court before the due date as and when the need arises. These are:

(a) **in adjourned proceedings**

- a first interim order may last for up to eight weeks beginning with the date on which it was made;

- a second or subsequent order may last for up to four weeks beginning with the date on which it was made or, where the first order was for less than 8 weeks, for up to 8 weeks from the date the first order was made. (So, if the first order was made for three weeks the second order could be made for up to 5 weeks; or, if the first and second orders were each made for one week, the third order could be made for up to 6 weeks. The 8 week threshold does not apply in reverse, i.e. where the first order is made for 5 weeks, say, the second order does not have to be limited to 3 weeks: The 4 week limit takes over.)

(b) **where in family proceedings a direction is given under section 37(1)**

- the end of the 8 week period or such other period as the court directs for the authority to report on its investigation (section 37(4)), subject to no care order or supervision order application having been made. (If an application is made and the proceedings on that application are adjourned, an interim order made then would be the second order and subject to the time limit for second and subsequent orders described above.)

(c) **General**

- an interim order ceases to have effect on disposal of the application for a care or supervision order.

3.46. The intention is that a more flexible initial time limit, backed by timetabling and reviews of progress, will expedite the final hearing. The court when deciding the timetabling of a case will nevertheless need satisfying on the need for a long interim order and it would not be expected that 4 week applications for subsequent orders would be made. Although there is no limit to the number of interim orders that can be made under the Act a balance will have to be struck between allowing sufficient time for enquiries, reports and statements, and risking allowing the child to continue in interim care or supervision for so long that the balance of advantage is distorted in favour of continued intervention. Subject to that, the emphasis should be very firmly on pressing on to a final hearing as quickly as possible (unless, of course, the matter can be resolved by negotiation without further compulsory intervention out of court). The guardian *ad litem* will have a key role in advising the court on interim orders – whether one should be made and if so which, for how long, whether directions are required on examinations and assessment, and on contact where an interim care order is made. The applicant should make his views known on these matters to the guardian *ad litem,* who will also want to establish the views of other parties including the child.

Directions on examination and assessment when an interim order is made

3.47. The Act gives the court a new power when making an interim care order or interim supervision order to give any directions it considers appropriate about medical or psychiatric examination or other assessment of the child (section 38(6)). The court can prohibit examination or assessment altogether or make this subject to its specific approval (section 38(7)). Directions can be given when the order is made or at any other time while it is in force. They are not appealable but may be varied on an application made in accordance with rules of court by any party who was a party to the proceedings in which the directions were given. Subsection (6) makes clear that if the child is of sufficient understanding he may refuse to submit to the examination or assessment.

3.48. The court has similar directions powers in support of the child assessment order (section 43(6)(b)) and emergency protection order (section 44(6)(b)). The court does not however have power to give directions when making a full care order (decisions on examinations and assessment fall within the local authority's parental responsibility, subject to the consent of a child of sufficient understanding); and its powers are more limited when a full supervision order is made. Paragraphs 4 and 5 of schedule 3 to the Act on psychiatric and medical examinations and treatment under a supervision order do not apply when an interim supervision order is made (section 38(9)); such matters have to be dealt with by court directions (though the court's power does not extend to treatment). These powers will allow the court to give attention to matters raised in the Cleveland Inquiry report, notably that children should not be subjected to repeated medical examinations solely for evidential purposes, and that where examination and interview is necessary they should be carried out in a suitable and sensitive environment with appropriately trained staff available. Local inter-agency arrangements should aim to establish a pool of health and other professionally trained experts who may be called on to participate in a wide-ranging programme of multi-disciplinary assessments and examinations. Considerations of the gender, ethnic and cultural identity of the child concerned will play a part in determining the programme of assessment and the manner in which it is undertaken.

3.49. An assessment, and maybe an examination, of the child will often be necessary as evidence showing whether the child is suffering, or is likely to suffer, significant harm – the first threshold condition for a full care or supervision order. In some cases this may have been carried out before the care or supervision proceedings, perhaps by agreement with the parents or under a child assessment order. In other cases the applicant should consider whether satisfactory arrangements can be made without the need for an interim order and court directions. He should try to discuss his proposals with the parents, the child (if of sufficient understanding) and the guardian *ad litem* before the adjourned hearing. The aim should be to secure the agreement of all concerned to a single programme of examination or assessment, which could if necessary be observed by, or conducted jointly with, a medical practitioner nominated by the parents. Parental agreement must always be balanced by the need to safeguard and protect the welfare of a child who may be at risk and this will mean ensuring that the assessment is carried out by those properly trained to do so. If the parents are co-operative, satisfactory arrangements can be made by agreement, and there is no immediate risk to the child's welfare, it may be unnecessary to seek an interim order and directions. If there are any doubts or where any aspect of the assessment is likely to prove contentious – for example, a possibility that if the examination found abuse the parents would want a second opinion requiring further examination of the child – the better course in the child's interests may be to seek an interim supervision order and court control by directions. The court will expect to be advised on these matters by the guardian *ad litem*, who will need to elicit the child's views and the positions of the applicant and the parents. In the last resort and where there is a conflict of views between the parties (the parents, the applicant and the guardian *ad litem*) the court must determine the type of assessment to be carried out and by whom based on the nature of the concern and what is in the best interests of the child.

3.50. Court directions on examinations or assessment do not override the right of the child who is of sufficient understanding to make an informed decision to refuse to submit to an examination or assessment. Examination or assessment without consent may be held in law to be an assault. For consent to be valid the person giving consent must be aware of what he or she is consenting to (and the possible consequences) and be freely given. A child of 16 is presumed in law to be capable of giving, or withholding, consent unless there is some mental incapacity to giving consent. Depending on their age and understanding, younger children may also be regarded by a doctor as capable of giving consent to examination or assessment. In all such cases it is the child's consent that is relevant, not that given by anyone else. Section 38(6) (and the similar provisions in sections 43 and 44) restate the position of the child of sufficient understanding in order to make clear beyond doubt that the child's consent is required even where the court makes directions. For younger children who are not regarded by a doctor as capable of giving consent, consent would normally have to be obtained from the parents. If an interim care order were made, the necessary parental responsibility would be acquired by the local authority, although the authority may have to use powers to restrict parents' exercise of parental responsibility. In other cases, for example where a specific issue arises and a private law section 8 order is sought, court directions could override the parents' ability to refuse consent.

3.51. The court will probably want to know, when considering giving directions on examination or assessment for the older child, whether the child is of sufficient age and understanding to give or withhold consent; if so, how he intends to respond; if there is any possibility of the child being put under pressure to refuse consent; and whether, as a result, the proposed order and directions are likely to be effective. The court will usually look to the guardian *ad litem* for advice on these matters. All have a duty to ensure that where the child is of sufficient age and understanding that his views are made known. Where a child's first language is not English, or where, because of a child's physical disability, communication methods other than speech and written language are necessary, expert assistance will be required to meet this responsibility. For a mentally handicapped child of sufficient age such assistance will be necessary to determine the child's capacity to understand. Directions by the court will not absolve the doctor or other person conducting the examination or assessment from his responsibility to satisfy himself that the child of sufficient age and understanding consents. He should not proceed if such consent is withheld. He should arrange for the facts of the matter to be reported to the court which gave the directions as soon as possible, usually via the guardian *ad litem*, so that the court may reconsider the direction. The interim order could be varied only on application by one of the parties.

Effects of, and responsibilities arising from, interim orders

3.52. By virtue of section 31(11) interim orders have the same effect and give the same responsibilities to local authorities as full orders, save for the differences noted in paragraph 3.38, namely that the court determines the length of the order and may give directions. In particular, the local authority acquires parental responsibility for the child for as long as the interim care order is in force. The new provisions on contact with the child also apply in interim care cases (section 34). (Interim supervision orders do not confer parental responsibility on the local authority and therefore contact with the child may only be controlled by a section 8 contact order.) Before making a section 34 order, the court must consider the local authority's proposals for contact and may invite the other parties to the proceedings to comment on them; and it may make an order under section 34 whether or not an application is made (see also paragraphs 3.75 – 3.86). The local authority's responsibilities following the making of an interim care order include reviewing the child's case in accordance with the Regulations made under section 26(1) and the rehabilitation duty in section 23(6). The Regulations require the authority when reviewing the case to consider whether to apply for discharge of the order and to inform the child of steps he may take under the Act. The authority should work for rehabilitation as soon as it is reasonably practicable and in the child's interests to do so according to the circumstances of the case. The temporary nature of the interim order should be allowed for in the exercise of these responsibilities, but it is not a reason for not taking them seriously.

3.53. It may very exceptionally arise that an authorised person obtains an interim care order without having been able to consult the local authority as required by section 31(6) – perhaps after emergency action when it is not immediately clear in which area the child is ordinarily resident. In these circumstances the authorised person may keep the child in his care but he and the designated local authority should arrange for the latter to take over care of the child as soon as possible. He would not have parental responsibility (a full or interim care order confers parental responsibility only on the designated local authority specified in the order) but would have actual care of the child and authority to do what is reasonable for safeguarding or promoting the child's welfare (section 3(5)). If it were necessary for the child to be accommodated overnight before the designated authority could take over his care, they could seek help from the authorised person or one of the authorities listed in section 27(3). Section 29(9) allows reimbursement of reasonable expenses incurred by another local authority in providing assistance.

DISCHARGE OF CARE ORDERS AND DISCHARGE AND VARIATION OF SUPERVISION ORDERS

3.54. Changes in the law governing applications for care and supervision orders are reflected in the new provisions for discharge of care orders and discharge or variation of supervision orders (section 39). (In line with the principle that management of compulsory care is the local authority's responsibility, the Act does not provide for variation of a care order.)

3.55. The child, local authority (care order) or supervisor (supervision order), and any person having parental responsibility for the child may apply for discharge or variation of the relevant order: in previous legislation parents and guardians could apply only if they had a separate representation order. Other persons with whom the child is living can apply for variation of a supervision order insofar as it affects them (section 39(3)). In previous legislation the court had to decide applications by reference to the imprecise test of whether it was appropriate to discharge the order; now, it must have regard to the welfare principles and checklist in section 1. The checklist should pick up any care and control needs the child may have which the court was specifically obliged to consider when considering discharge of a care order under previous legislation. The court can deal with an application for discharge of a care order by substituting a supervision order without having to re-establish the section 31(2) grounds. The previous findings of fact in relation to the significant harm condition will be treated as accepted findings in the new application to discharge the care order. The court's concern will focus on what, if any, alternative provisions can be made to safeguard and promote the welfare of the child. Unlike in previous legislation the reverse provision does not apply. A care order can be made where the child was subject to a supervision order only after a fresh finding that the conditions for such an order are satisfied after a full hearing under section 31. This is so even though the application will most likely arise from non-compliance with the terms of the original supervision order.

3.56. A further change giving greater flexibility is that a care order is automatically discharged by the making of a residence order (section 91(1)). This route extends opportunities to bring a care order to an end to the following persons not having parental responsibility: local authority foster parents (if they satisfy the conditions in section 9(3)), an unmarried father (section 10(5)(a)), any person with whom the child has lived for at least three years (section 10(5)(b)), any person who has the consent of the local authority to apply for a residence order (section 10(5)(c)(ii)) and any person who succeeds in an application for leave to bring an application (section 10(9)). When considering an application for leave, the court has to have regard, *inter alia*, to the local authority's plans for the child's future and the wishes and feelings of the child's parents. A person in whose favour a residence order is made, and who thereby acquires parental responsibility if he does not already have it, is able to apply for discharge or variation of a supervision order under section 39(2)(a).

3.57. Local authorities are required by the Review of Children's Cases Regulations 1991 made under section 26(2) to consider at least at every statutory review of a case of a child in local authority care whether to apply for discharge of the care order. As part of each review the child has to be informed of steps he may take himself, which include applying for discharge of the order, applying for a contact order or variation of an existing contact order or for leave to apply for a residence order (section 10(8)). The authority should also work in suitable cases towards bringing a care order to an end through rehabilitation of the child under section 23(6) (see Volume 3). The authority should prepare for his rehabilitation by advising, assisting and befriending him under section 24 and, if appropriate, by encouraging increased contact with the person or persons concerned (applying if necessary for variation of an order made under section 34). The court does not have power to postpone discharge of a care order to allow for a gradual return of the child to his family over a period of time. However it can encourage the process of rehabilitation by varying the contact provisions consistent with a plan for return. It can also make a residence order with appropriate directions and conditions under section 11(7) coupled with a supervision order.

3.58. The supervisor of a child under a supervision order must consider whether or not to apply for the order to be varied or discharged where it is not wholly complied with or he considers that the order may no longer be necessary (see also paragraphs 3.87-3.97 below). Cases of non-compliance can include cases where a child of sufficient understanding refuses consent to a medical or psychiatric examination (or treatment) required by the order. The supervisor should also review the need for, and reasonableness of, any directions he has given to the child or responsible person under the order, the arrangements made for carrying them out, and whether it would be in the interests of the child to change these. In considering whether to make application to the court, he should consider how the court would be likely to view the application using the checklist in section 1(3).

3.59. The Act places a time limit on repeat applications (section 91(15) and (16)). Where an application for discharge of a care order or supervision order or to substitute a supervision order for a care order has been disposed of, no further application of this kind may be made within six months without leave of the court. This does not apply to interim orders or applications to vary a supervision order.

APPEALS AGAINST CARE AND SUPERVISION ORDERS

3.60. Rules of court provide that any one who had party status in the original proceedings may appeal against the making of a care or supervision order (including an interim order) or of an order varying or discharging such an order, or against the court's refusal to make such an order. This is an improvement on the position in previous legislation, when the child had a general right of appeal but the parents could appeal in their own right only where a separate representation order had been made. Local authorities, like any other party, have full rights of appeal. Decisions by a magistrates' court are appealable to the High Court (section 94(1)), instead of to the Crown Court as under previous legislation. Appeals against decisions in care or supervision proceedings heard in the county court or High Court will continue to go to the Court of Appeal (section 77(1) of the County Courts Act 1984 and section 16 of the Supreme Court Act 1981.)

3.61. For the first time, primary legislation sets out the court's order-making powers pending an appeal in specific circumstances in care or supervision proceedings (section 40). The circumstances are where there is already some background of compulsory intervention in the child's upbringing. The court can exercise these powers when an intention to appeal is notified or when an appeal can be made but is still being considered. The basic approach is to allow the immediate *status quo* to be maintained in order to provide continued protection for the child or to prevent interruption in the continuity of his care until the appeal is heard.

3.62. Thus, where the court dismisses an application for a care order and the child is at that time subject to an interim care order, the court may make a care order pending the appeal. If it dismisses an application for a care order or an application for a supervision order and the child is at that time subject to an interim supervision order, the court may make a supervision order pending the appeal. In each case the court can include directions in the order on any matter to do with the child's welfare that it considers appropriate. Where the court agrees to discharge a care or supervision order it may order that pending the appeal the decision is not to have effect, or that the order should remain in force subject to any directions it makes. These are the only circumstances, except in relation to contact, in which the court on its own initiative can involve itself by giving directions in management of the welfare of the child in compulsory care.

3.63. These orders may be extended by an appeal court where an appeal is lodged against a decision of another court with respect to an order pending appeal. However orders made under this section can only have effect until the date the appeal is determined or, where no appeal is made, the period during which it could be made expires. Furthermore, if the court makes a residence order in care or supervision proceedings, it can postpone the coming into effect of the order or impose temporary requirements pending an appeal under section 11(7).

3.64. Continuation of the proceedings may itself be unsettling for the child; the court must continue to have regard to the presumption against making an order in section 1(5) and will need persuading that a pending-appeal order is required. The court's timetable for the case will need extending to provide for the appeal and should reflect the need to bring the proceedings to a conclusion as quickly as possible.

EFFECT OF CARE ORDERS

3.65. Section 33 of the Act defines the legal effect of a care order (including, by virtue of section 31(11), an interim care order), whether made in care proceedings or in other family proceedings. It clarifies the relationship between the local authority's and parents' responsibilities for the child in care, and removes inconsistencies in the effect of orders made in different proceedings under previous legislation. These provisions establish a legal foundation for the local authority's welfare responsibilities towards children in care in Part III of the Act. The effects of the making of a care order on other orders are set out in section 91.

3.66. The local authority designated by the care order is responsible for looking after the child (see section 31(8)). They must provide accommodation for him and maintain him in accordance with section 23; safeguard and promote his welfare (section 22(3)(a)); and give effect to or act in accordance with the other welfare responsibilities in sections 22 to 26 and Part II of schedule 2 (see Volume 3).

3.67. The designated local authority acquires parental responsibility for the child for as long as the order is in force. It also has power to determine the extent to which parents or guardians (who do not lose their parental responsibility on the making of the order) may meet their responsibility. This new power marks the principal difference in the positions on parental responsibility under a care order and residence order (section 12). It allows the local authority to deal with any conflict that may arise between the authority and the parents in exercising their respective parental responsibilities.

3.68. Section 2(7) allows any person with parental responsibility to act alone and without others in meeting that responsibility. This is subject to the caveat in section 2(8) that a person with parental responsibility may not act in a way which would be incompatible with an order made under the Act. However, there could be arguments as to whether a proposed action of which the authority disapproved was incompatible with the care order. The authority can use their power but only if they are satisfied that it is necessary to do so in order to safeguard or promote the child's welfare. Where a local authority intend to limit the way in which a parent meets his responsibility this should be discussed with the parent and incorporated in the plan of arrangements for the child whilst in care so that it may be subject to periodic review. Note that exercising this power does not prevent a parent or guardian who has care of the child on a weekend visit, for example, from doing what is reasonable to safeguard or promote his welfare.

3.69. A parent or guardian also retains any rights, duties, powers, responsibilities or authority in relation to the child and his property which they have under other legislation – for example, the right to consent or refuse to consent to the child's marriage, rights under the Education Act 1981 in relation to the child's special educational needs, financial responsibility for the child. (However, under amendments to the Marriage Act 1949, the authority's consent for the marriage of a child in care who is 16 or 17 is needed).

3.70. Subject to the specific restrictions in section 33 (see below), the local authority have all the rights, duties, powers, responsibilities and authority to act as parent of the child in care and to discharge all their responsibilities to him positively and effectively. These include having to decide how to best care for him in accordance with section 33. They may not transfer any part of their parental responsibility to someone else, but can arrange for some or all of it to be met on their behalf by others (e.g. a local authority foster parent or a voluntary organisation).

3.71. Section 33 prevents the local authority doing certain things by virtue of their parental responsibility; most are carried forward from previous legislation. They must not cause the child to be brought up in any religious persuasion other that in which he would have been brought up had the order not been made. This does not prevent the child determining his own religious beliefs as he grows older; it simply requires the local authority not to bring about any change by their own action or inaction. They should not, for example, place a child who has been brought up in a particular religion with a foster parent who, deliberately or by omission, would be likely to prevent the child continuing to practice his beliefs for as long as he wished.

3.72. The local authority may not consent, or refuse to consent, to an application for a freeing for adoption order; or agree, or refuse to agree, to an adoption order or proposed foreign adoption order. The authority also cannot appoint a guardian for the child, which now must always be done in accordance with section 5.

3.73. The authority may not change the child's surname or remove him from the United Kingdom without written consent of every parent or guardian who has parental responsibility for the child, or leave of the court to do so. The jurisdiction on removal does not apply where it is for less than one month (for example, to allow him to go on holiday abroad with his foster parents or to visit relatives abroad), or to arrangements for the child to live abroad approved by the court under paragraph 19 of Schedule 2.

3.74. Under section 91, the making of a care order discharges any section 8 order (including a residence order), supervision order or school attendance order to which the child was subject at the time the care order was made. It also brings any wardship to an end. If an emergency protection order is made while the child is subject to a care order (this may be necessary if a serious situation arises during a placement), the care order can be 'trumped' by the emergency protection order to allow the holder of the emergency protection order to take whatever action he considers necessary to protect the child.

CONTACT WITH CHILDREN IN CARE

3.75. Guidance in paragraphs 3.76 – 3.86 below should be read in conjunction with guidance on practice and Regulations contained in Volume 2.

3.76. Section 34 introduces major new provisions on contact with children in care. It establishes that a local authority must allow reasonable contact with his parents and certain other people, unless directed otherwise by a court order, or the local authority temporarily suspend contact in urgent circumstances. It requires the court to consider contact arrangements before making a care order and gives it wide powers to deal with problems. The underlying principle is that the authority, child and other persons concerned should as far as possible agree reasonable arrangements before the care order is made, but should be able to seek the court's assistance if agreement cannot be reached or the authority want to deny contact to a person who is entitled to it under the Act. These provisions substantially improve the position of parents and others seeking contact compared with previous legislation, and limit the authority's power to control and deny contact. However, it should be recognised that there will be cases where contact will be detrimental to the child's welfare. This possibility should be considered at the pre-court proceedings stage, when plans for contact are being drawn up. Applications for orders prohibiting contact are discussed at paragraph 3.81 below.

3.77. The presumption that contact is allowed for certain named people, and the pro-active role given to the court reflect the importance of this subject. Regular contact with parents, relatives and friends will usually be an important part of the child's upbringing in his new environment and is essential to successful rehabilitation. Lack of contact can, over a period, have vital consequences for the rights of parents and children; it can be a major factor in deciding whether to discharge a care order or to dispense with parental agreement to adoption. This is too important to be regarded as simply a matter of management within the sole control of the local authority. The new scheme is intended to provide a basis for good practice and remove the perceived unfairness in previous arrangements. It is separate from the contact provisions in Part II of the Act; a section 8 contact order cannot be made when a child is in local authority care (section 9(1)), and an existing order is automatically discharged on the making of a care order (section 91(2)).

3.78. The authority is required to allow the child reasonable contact with his parents, any guardian, and any person having the benefit of a residence order or care of the child under wardship immediately before the care order was made (on the making of which the residence order or wardship lapses). The parent includes an unmarried father. Subject to any court order, it is for the authority to decide what is reasonable contact in the circumstances. The degree of contact should not necessarily remain static; the local authority may plan for the frequency or duration of contact to increase or decrease over time. Again this should be specified in the plan which is prepared and submitted to the court prior to the making of an order. Where possible, the plan should have been discussed with the child and his parents; any disagreements can be resolved by the court making an order as to the degree of contact.

3.79. There are a number of ways in which the local authority's proposals for contact may be scrutinised or challenged:

(a) the court, before making the care order, must consider the arrangements made or proposed by the authority and ask parties to the proceedings to comment on them (section 34 (11)). The guardian *ad litem* is also likely to comment on the arrangements with the child's interests in mind;

(b) any person to whom the Act's presumption of reasonable contact applies, or any other person who has obtained the leave of the court, can apply for an order about contact at any time if he is dissatisfied with the arrangements made or proposed for contact between the child and himself;

(c) the child can do the same, and can also apply for his contact with another person to be reduced, suspended or terminated;

(d) the court, if it is satisfied that it should do so under section 1(5), can make any order about contact that it considers appropriate either in response to an application or on its own initiative, and can impose any conditions it considers appropriate. The conditions can be as specific as the court judges necessary, for example, that contact is supervised or takes place at a particular time or place, or is reviewed at prescribed intervals.

judges necessary, for example, that contact is supervised or takes place at a particular time or place, or is reviewed at prescribed intervals.

3.80. The local authority has the same powers as the child to apply for a court order, and can also refuse contact that would otherwise be required by virtue of the statutory entitlement or a court order for a limited period without reference to the court. They must be satisfied that this is necessary in order to safeguard or promote the child's welfare, and the refusal must be decided upon as a matter of urgency and not last for more than seven days. The person concerned or the child may apply to the court for an order in response to such a decision. If the authority considers it necessary to refuse contact for a longer period they must apply for an order under section 34(4), whereupon under rules of court the person concerned and the child may contest the application. The authority, child or person named in the order may apply at any time for an order to be varied or discharged; and any party to the proceedings (including the local authority) can appeal against the making of, or refusal to make, an order.

3.81. Action to set aside contact under section 34(6) is a serious step which should not be undertaken lightly. That said, the authority should not hesitate to use this power if contact with a particular person or persons proves harmful or potentially harmful to the child's welfare. There must however be some sudden new circumstance or rapid deterioration in relations with the child to justify deciding the refusal as a matter of urgency. If a problem can be seen developing over a period, the proper course for the authority is to try to negotiate a reduction or even termination of contact and, if that does not succeed, to apply for an order (and, if necessary, conditions) under either section 34(2) or 34(4) or, if an order already exists, for variation or discharge under section 34(9). Regulation 3 of the Contact with Children Regulations 1991 outlines the actions which the local authority are required to take before they can depart from the terms of a court order on contact. If agreement cannot be reached, and the conditions outlined in section 34(6) (enabling the local authority to temporarily suspend contact in order to safeguard the child's welfare – see paragraph 3.80 above) do not apply, the local authority will have to consider applying to the court for an order restricting contact.

3.82. Section 34(6) applies only to situations where the local authority wishes to refuse contact to a person to whom the presumption of reasonable contact under section 34(1) applies, or who is the beneficiary of an order. However, there may also be occasions or circumstances where it is important to refuse contact to a person who is not entitled to contact, but has nevertheless been having contact with the child. In such cases it may be helpful to apply the principle outlined in section 34(6) – that contact should only be denied in order to safeguard or promote the child's welfare. The local authority can invoke their care management duties in such cases; contact should be refused immediately in urgent circumstances, but in general, and to ensure consistency in the refusal of contact, the requirements of section 34(6) should be satisfied. In non-urgent cases, the local authority should give the person concerned notice of their intention to end contact between that person and the child. This should be discussed with the child if he is of sufficient age and understanding. The person concerned should be provided with details of the representations procedure (see Volume 3), and informed of their right to apply to the court for leave to make an application for an order under section 34(3). If agreement cannot be reached, particularly if the person had previously enjoyed contact with the child, the authority should apply for an order as quickly as possible or encourage the person concerned to do so, so that the impact of refusal of contact on the child can be tested by the court.

3.83. Repeat applications for orders under section 34 are controlled by section 91(17). If an application for an order has been refused, the person concerned may not re-apply for the same order in respect of the same child within six months without court leave. The court would expect to hear of a change in circumstances sufficient to justify a departure from this rule, which is designed to discourage frequent rehearings of the same case. The local authority is not exempt from this restriction; it, however, will be expected to carry out good child care practice, seeking the leave of the court to vary or discharge a contact order as appropriate. The court also has a more general power under section 91(14) to prevent applications being made without the leave of the court.

3.84. Certain other provisions in the Act bear on the question of contact (paragraph 15 of schedule 2). The authority have a general duty to promote contact between the child and his parents, others who have parental responsibility and relatives, friends and others. They must take reasonable steps to keep certain of these people informed of his whereabouts, unless the authority have reasonable cause for believing that giving that information would be prejudicial to the child's welfare. Information must also be given where another authority take over the provision of accommodation. Information about the child may only be withheld where it is essential to the welfare of the child, and where the child is in the care of the local authority by virtue of an order under section 31. If the child is being looked after on a voluntary basis, the provisions of paragraph 15(4) of schedule 2 *do not apply*, and the local authority is not entitled to withhold information. Where the authority provides accommodation, including the placing of the child with a local authority foster parent they must try to ensure that the accommodation is near his home, so that contact is facilitated.

3.85. The local authority may make payments to assist contact (paragraph 16 of schedule 2); this is intended mainly to help with costs incurred in making visits. This help may be given to the parent (or other person who is entitled to contact with the child) or to the child. The general duty of a local authority to promote contact between a child and his parents should be borne in mind when determining whether such assistance should be provided. Thus the local authority should ensure that the parents and child are aware that such assistance is available when plans for contact are being discussed.

3.86. Children with special needs, or who have difficulty in communicating, may need extra local authority support to help them to maintain contact when placed at a distance from their home area. Contact includes communication by letter and telephone, and some children may need special provisions to facilitate this type of contact. Particular consideration must also be given to the needs of children for whom their first language (or that of their parent) is not English. Again, plans for contact should include the arrangements which the local authority proposes to make in respect of the particular needs of the child in question.

SUPERVISION ORDERS

3.87. Supervision orders and interim supervision orders have for the most part been dealt with in the preceding sections of this guidance – those on the court's order-making powers, applications, criteria for orders, court directions and variation and discharge of orders, for example – where the provisions are common to both supervision orders and care orders or raise common points. The following paragraphs deal more specifically with supervision orders and section 35 and Parts I and II of schedule 3.

3.88. A supervision order puts the child under the supervision of a designated local authority or a probation officer in accordance with paragraph 9 of schedule 3. The supervisor is given three specific duties in section 35:

(a) to advise, assist and befriend the child;

(b) to take all reasonable steps to see that the order is given effect; and

(c) to consider whether to apply for variation or discharge of the order where it is not being wholly complied with or he considers that the order may no longer be necessary.

The supervisor must also refer back to the court on medical treatment in accordance with paragraph 5(6) of schedule 3 should the need arise. The duty to "advise, assist and befriend" restates the requirements of the Children and Young Persons Act 1969, and imposes no new duties on the supervisor.

3.89. The principal change from previous legislation is that requirements may be imposed on a responsible person, who is defined in paragraph 1 of schedule 3 as any person with parental responsibility for the child, or any other person with whom he is living. Under previous legislation, the inability of the court or supervisor to require the parents or other responsible adult to contribute towards making the supervision order effective, or even to allow access to the child, was often an important factor in the perceived ineffectiveness of supervision orders. The new scheme provides a number of new powers, which may require the child to:

(a)   live at a place specified in directions given by the supervisor;

(b)   take part in education or training activities;

(c)   report to particular places at particular times;

(d)   submit to psychiatric or medical examination or treatment (under court directions in the case of an interim supervision order, if this is required for health and development and/or evidential purposes);

(e)   make himself available for monitoring visits by the supervisor at the place where he is living.

It should be noted that the court cannot make a direction requiring the child to submit to psychiatric or medical examination or treatment unless the child, if of sufficient understanding to do so, consents to its inclusion in the order. The local authority should always consider very carefully when contemplating an application under section 31 whether these powers, including the power of the court and supervisor to impose requirements on a responsible person or persons, are sufficient to promote and safeguard the welfare of the child. The court and guardian *ad litem* will certainly wish to do so.

3.90. The requirements which may be made of the supervised child or responsible person are set out in detail in schedule 3; this replaces detailed provisions in previous legislation with tighter provisions on examinations and treatment, the length of supervision orders and the new power to impose requirements on responsible persons. Requirements as to treatment are wholly the responsibility of the court and have to be specified in the order itself (paragraph 5). Requirements as to examinations may be specified by the court in the order or by the supervisor (paragraph 4).

3.91. Other matters are for the supervisor, provided the supervision order contains the necessary authority – his power to give directions to the child as to where he should live, on reporting to a person and place and on participating in activities (paragraph 2); directions to the responsible person (paragraph 3(1)(c)); and requirements on the child and responsible person to provide information and allow visiting (paragraph 8). The court can also require the responsible person through the supervision order to take all reasonable steps to ensure that the child complies with requirements and directions under paragraphs 2, 4 and 5. The responsible person has to consent to requirements of himself being included in the order; his co-operation is a vital contribution to the effectiveness of the order.

3.92. Paragraphs 4 and 5 of schedule 3 deal with the important questions of health examinations and treatment at some length, and they include several new provisions. The child may be required to submit to a medical or psychiatric examination by the court through the order or by direction of the supervisor if the order gives authority for this. The arrangements for the examination must be in accordance with paragraph 4(2) and (3) of the schedule. It may be carried out at a hospital or mental nursing home with the child attending as a resident patient only if the court is satisfied by medical evidence that the child requires treatment and may be susceptible to it, and that it is necessary for him to stay as a resident patient. The court must in all cases be satisfied that, if the child is of sufficient understanding to make an informed decision, he consents to the inclusion of these requirements, and that the arrangements will be satisfactory.

3.93. Paragraph 5 on treatment requires all directions to be given by the court, not the supervisor, and it imposes different conditions for directions on psychiatric treatment (paragraph 5(1) and (2)) and physical treatment (paragraph 5(3) and (4)). The court has to be satisfied, on the basis of advice from clinical experts, that the treatment is needed and it must specify in the order how it is to be provided. The same requirements regarding consent apply in the case of treatment as apply to examination: If the child is of sufficient understanding he must consent to the inclusion of the direction in the order.

3.94. The medical practitioner responsible for the treatment must report in writing to the supervisor if he is unwilling for the treatment to continue for any reason, or if he considers that the treatment should continue beyond the period specified, the child needs different treatment, he is not susceptible to treatment or does not require further treatment. The supervisor must refer the report to the court, which may then cancel or vary its requirements as to treatment.

3.95. As in previous legislation, there is no prescribed remedy for breach of a requirement or direction; the supervisor would have to consider, where the order is not wholly complied with, whether to apply to the court for its variation or discharge (section 35(3)). If the supervisor is prevented from visiting the child or having reasonable contact with him under paragraphs 8(1)(b) and (2)(b) of schedule 3, he may apply to the court for a warrant under section 102. The warrant is intended to enable the person concerned to exercise his powers. If the supervisor considered that the refusal of reasonable contact requires that urgent action be taken, he should consider whether to apply for for an emergency protection order or ask the constable to take the child into police protection under section 46. Failure to comply with requirements may lead to the local authority reconsidering its plans for the child, and this possibility should be explained to the child, the responsible person and his parents, and to any other person caring for the child, so that they know where they stand and can see the value to the child of their co-operation. The local authority should at all times respond to non co-operation in a positive and constructive way designed to regain that co-operation. Failure to work closely with those concerned with the child's welfare, in particular with the parents, may lead to a breakdown in the local authority's relationship with the parents, and consequent deleterious effects on the welfare of the child. The aim must be at all times to strive to gain the parent's support for the plans for the child's future. The court and guardian *ad litem* are also likely to want to ensure that the child and other persons understand the significance of the order when it is made.

3.96. Subject to its not being brought to an end earlier, a supervision order will last for one year in the first instance (paragraph 6 of schedule 3). This represents a change from previous legislation, which allowed the court to specify a period not exceeding three years. The supervisor can apply for an extension, or further extensions, for any period subject to the order not running for more than 3 years beyond the original date. The new one-year time limit is intended to ensure that after a reasonable period the effectiveness of the order and the circumstances of the child are reviewed and a decision taken about further steps, if any, with the child, parents and others concerned being given the opportunity to participate in further proceedings if necessary. A supervision order is brought to an end by the court discharging the order, the making of a care order with respect to the child, the child reaching the age of 18 (section 91) or if a court takes action under section 25(1)(a) of the Child Abduction and Custody Act 1985 – by making an order for the return of the child under part I of that Act – or section 25(1)(b) where a decision with respect to the child is registered under Part 16 of that Act. The making of a supervision order brings to an end a live care or supervision order which had been made earlier – as with the care order referred to above the later order 'trumps' the first. An interim supervision order may accompany a residence order in the circumstances described in section 38(3) (see paragraph 3.41 above).

3.97. The Act makes a number of related changes. The family assistance order which the court may make in family proceedings under section 16 (see paragraphs 2.50 – 2.53) in part replaces the supervision order which could be made in divorce, wardship, adoption and other proceedings under previous legislation where there were exceptional circumstances making supervision desirable. The court may make a family assistance order in care or supervision proceedings, these being family proceedings, and the provisions of section 16 will apply equally in these cases as in divorce, custody, adoption etc. cases. In future a supervision order can be made in family proceedings only if the criteria in sections 31(2) or 38(2) are satisfied. A supervision order may still be made in criminal proceedings under the now quite separate code in the Children and Young Persons Act 1969; this has different conditions and effects, and new provisions for attaching a residence requirement in certain circumstances have been added.

WARDSHIP AND THE INHERENT JURISDICTION OF THE HIGH COURT

3.98. The impact of the Children Act on the inherent jurisdiction of the High Court will be considerable. By incorporating many of the beneficial aspects of wardship, such as the 'open door' policy, and a flexible range of orders, the Act will substantially reduce the need to have recourse to the High Court. But in addition there is a specific prohibition against using the inherent jurisdiction in general, and wardship in particular, as an alternative to public law orders. Without this prohibition, the threshold criteria which have been carefully designed as the minimum circumstances justifying state intervention would be undermined, as too would any directions attached to these orders (such as to their duration or other effects). Where a wardship court thinks that a care or supervision order may be needed, it may direct a local authority to investigate the child's circumstances and, if the statutory conditions are satisfied, make an interim care or supervision order. These are the same powers that are available to any court in family proceedings. Similarly, since proceedings under the inherent jurisdiction are family proceedings it is open to the court to make a section 8 order.

3.99. The Act also affects the relationship between wardship and local authority care. Under the old law it was possible for a child in compulsory care also to be a ward of court. Wardship in these circumstances could only be invoked with the local authority's agreement. An exception arose where a ward of court was committed to care under section 7(2) of the Family Law Reform Act 1969 and the court retained the power to give directions to the local authority on the application of others such as the child's parents. While the child was a ward of court, the local authority's powers were uncertain because, in wardship, the court is said to be the child's guardian. The local authority's powers were restricted by the rule which required major decisions in the child's life to be referred to the court. Where the child is in care this division of responsibility should not occur. The local authority has parental responsibility for the child and should be able to take whatever decisions are necessary. The Act therefore makes wardship and care incompatible. If a ward of court is committed to care the wardship ceases to have effect (section 91(4)). While a child is in care he cannot be made a ward of court (section 100(2) and section 41 of the Supreme Court Act 1981 as amended by paragraph 45 of schedule 13).

3.100. The inherent jurisdiction remains available as a remedy of last resort where a local authority seeks the resolution of a specific issue concerning the future of a child in its care. But there are restrictions: The first is that the local authority must have the High Court's leave to apply for the exercise of its inherent jurisdiction (section 100(3)). Leave may only be granted where the court is satisfied that the local authority could not achieve the desired result through the making of any order other than one under the inherent jurisdiction. Where there are statutory remedies within the Act, the local authority will be expected to pursue those. In particular, where a child is not in local authority care, the local authority will rarely be granted leave since they could otherwise obtain a specific issue or prohibited steps order under section 8. An exception might be where the local authority seek to restrain publicity about the child. Second, even where there is no other statutory remedy within the Act, there must be reasonable cause to believe that the child is likely to suffer significant harm if the inherent jurisdiction is not exercised.

3.101. Since the local authority will have parental responsibility for children in their care they should make decisions themselves in consultation with the parents as appropriate and after taking the child's views into account. Nevertheless there may be occasions where recourse to the High Court is appropriate as the decisions to be taken are highly contentious, and/or fall far outside the normal scope of decision-making for children in care. An example might be the sterilisation of a child in care. Other less extreme situations may also merit High Court intervention, for example, to restrain harmful publicity about the child. In such cases when the inherent jurisdiction is the only means of obtaining the remedy, it should not be too difficult to satisfy the leave criteria.

3.102. The Act further prevents the High Court from exercising its inherent jurisdiction "for the purposes of conferring on any local authority power to determine any question which has arisen, or which may arise in connection with any aspect of parental responsibility". Thus, in making an order under its inherent jurisdiction, the court cannot confer on the local authority any degree of parental responsibility it does not already have (section 100(2)).

3.103. On commencement (schedule 14 paragraph 15 as amended by the Courts and Legal Services Act 1990 schedule 16 paragraph 33) any orders made under the Family Law Reform Act 1969 section 7(2) and in the exercise of the High Court's inherent jurisdiction committing wards of court into local authority care are deemed to be care orders as defined by the Children Act, and the child will cease to be a ward of court. However, any directions made prior to commencement of the Act will effectively become 'free-standing' and remain in force until varied or discharged by the court. As soon after commencement as is reasonably practicable local authorities will wish to seek a discharge or variation of these directions where they appear to unduly fetter the local authority's exercise of their parental responsibility and hamper effective management of a child in their care. They will also need to consider whether to seek the conversion of care orders triggered by the transitional provisions into other orders. The High Court's intention in making the original order will be one of the factors the local authority should take into account. For example, where a child, prior to commencement of the Act, was in the care and control of the local authority by virtue of the High Court's inherent jurisdiction but placed with the child's own family, a residence order coupled with a supervision order might provide a more appropriate remedy.

CHAPTER 4   **PROTECTION OF CHILDREN**

4.1. Part V of the Act fundamentally recasts the law on protecting children at risk to ensure that effective protective action can be taken when this is necessary within a framework of proper safeguards and reasonable opportunities for parents and others connected with the child to challenge such actions before a court. The measures are short-term and time-limited, and may or may not lead to further action under Parts III or IV. It is therefore essential that guidance in Volumes 2 and 3 is kept in mind*.

4.2. Local authorities are given more positive duties to investigate cases of suspected child abuse and decide what action is appropriate, supported by a new duty on other authorities to give assistance if asked to do so. For emergencies, the place of safety order is replaced by an emergency protection order with new stricter grounds, clearly defined responsibilities for the person holding the order and shorter time limits. In other cases where significant harm is suspected and attempts to have the child examined or assessed by voluntary arrangement have failed, a new child assessment order is available. Police powers to detain a child for protection purposes have been redefined to fit into the new scheme, and so have powers of entry and search. Finally, provisions on abduction and recovery of children who are the subject of compulsory intervention have been amended and an updated recovery order introduced. There are new provisions, too, for recognising homes which provide refuges for children at risk.

4.3. The new provisions for emergencies are intended to address matters which have caused difficulties in the past. The grounds for the emergency protection order address more clearly the purpose of having power to remove the child. This differs from the old place of safety order where the grounds were more loosely framed, and could be used in situations which were not always strictly an emergency, for example, as a means of starting care proceedings. The new grounds provide, in particular, for cases where attempts to see a child about whom there is serious concern have been unreasonably frustrated. The duration and effect of the order is limited to what is necessary to protect the child. The parents and certain others will be able to challenge the making of an order if present at the hearing or, if they were not, ask the court to discharge the order after 72 hours.

4.4. The child assessment order is emphatically not for emergencies. It is a lesser, heavily court-controlled order dealing with the narrow issue of examination or assessment of the child in specific circumstances of non co-operation by the parents and lack of evidence of the need for a different type of order or other action.

4.5. Proceedings under Part V are not classified as family proceedings for the purpose of the Act. This means that in these proceedings the court must either make or refuse to make the order applied for and cannot make any other kind of order. The only exception is the court's specific authority to make an emergency protection order instead of a child assessment order. The court must however have regard to the overriding principle that the child's welfare is paramount (section 1(1)) and the presumption of no order (section 1(5)). Though the court

---

*This Chapter uses references to 'parents' in relation to the carers of children in respect of whom orders under Part V may be sought, but it applies equally to carers even though such persons will often not have parental responsibility

is not required to consider the checklist of relevant factors (section 1(3)) (because in an emergency the necessary information would be unlikely to be available) such consideration should be given as far as is reasonably practicable. Applications for emergency protection orders may be made *ex-parte* and no appeal may be made against the making of, or refusal to make, an emergency protection order, or the extension of, the discharge of and any directions made under, an emergency protection order. Apart from these differences, these provisions generally follow the main principles and approaches of other court- and local authority-related provisions in the Act. For example, the procedures for other types of proceedings in the new system of concurrent jurisdiction will be followed as closely as possible; the grounds for the two main orders, like those of the main compulsory intervention orders in part IV, are based on present or anticipated significant harm; and notification, contact, consent to examinations and limiting the length of the order to the minimum necessary are all emphasised. The protection provisions have been integrated into the general scheme of the Act as fully as possible.

CHILD ASSESSMENT ORDERS

4.6. The child assessment order, established by section 43, had no parallel in previous legislation. It deals with the single issue of enabling an assessment of the child to be made where significant harm is suspected but the child is not thought to be at immediate risk (requiring his removal, or keeping him in hospital), the local authority or authorised person considers that an assessment is required, and the parents or other persons responsible for him have refused to co-operate. Its purpose is to allow the local authority or authorised person to ascertain enough about the state of the child's health or development or the way in which he has been treated to decide what further action, if any, is required. It is less interventionist than the emergency protection order, interim care order and interim supervision order and should not be used where the circumstances of the case suggest that one of these orders would be more appropriate. The court has power to make an emergency protection order instead of the child assessment order if, after hearing the evidence, it considers that the circumstances warrant this (section 43(4)).

Applications

4.7. Only a local authority or 'authorised' person may apply for a child assessment order; in this limitation it is similar to care and supervision orders but not emergency protection orders, for which anyone may apply to the court (see paragraphs 4.32 and 4.45 below). The court has to be satisfied on each of the following three conditions:

 — *that the applicant has reasonable cause to* suspect *that the child is suffering, or is likely to suffer, significant harm.*

 — *that an assessment of the state of the child's health and development, or of the way he has been treated, is required to enable the applicant to determine whether or not the child is suffering, or is likely to suffer, significant harm.*

 — *that it is unlikely that such an assessment will be made or be satisfactory in the absence of a child assessment order.*

Finally, as with all orders made under this Act, the court must give regard to the child's welfare as paramount and be satisfied that making the order would be better for the child than making no order at all.

Conditions to be satisfied

4.8. The principal conditions are very specific. The order is for cases where there are suspicions, but no firm evidence, of actual or likely significant harm in circumstances which do not constitute an emergency; the applicant considers that a decisive step to obtain an assessment is needed to show whether the concern is well founded or further action is not required, and that informal arrangements to have such an assessment carried out have failed. For example, the parents or other persons looking after the child have resisted attempts to arrange an examination or assessment by agreement or failed to bring the child to see a doctor when arrangements have been made, and have not made suitable alternative arrangements. The problem may have come to light from contact with the family or child by a health visitor, social worker, doctor, teacher or other professional, or from a concerned relative or neighbour.

4.9. A child assessment order will usually be most appropriate where the harm to the child is long-term and cumulative rather than sudden and severe. The circumstances may be nagging concern about a child who appears to be failing to thrive; or the parents are ignorant of or unwilling to face up to possible harm to their child because of the state of his health or development; or it appears that the child may be subject to wilful neglect or abuse but not to such an extent as to place him at serious immediate risk. Sexual abuse, which covers a wide range of behaviour, can fall in this category: The harm to the child can be long-term rather than immediate and it does not necessarily require emergency action. However, emergency action should not be avoided where disclosure of the abuse is itself likely to put the child at immediate risk of significant harm and/or where there is an urgent need to gather particular forensic evidence which would not otherwise be forthcoming in relation to the likelihood of significant harm.

4.10. One of the essential ingredients for a child assessment order is that an assessment is needed to help establish basic facts about the child's condition. Because information is lacking it is unlikely that an interim care or supervision order could be obtained and an examination or assessment arranged under those provisions: the condition for an interim order – "reasonable grounds for believing that the circumstances are as mentioned in section 31(2)" – section 38(2) (see paragraphs 3.36 and 3.37) is more demanding and would be difficult to satisfy. However, the applicant should know enough of the circumstances to satisfy himself that the child is not in immediate danger; if possible the child should have been seen recently by someone competent to judge this. A skilled social work practitioner would be in a position to make a judgement as to the child's emotional state and to obvious changes in the child's physical well-being. Finer judgements, particularly in relation to very young children, may require input from the child's health visitor, GP or other health professional. Refusal to allow a child about whom there is serious concern to be seen (as opposed to being examined or assessed) can be a classic sign of a potential emergency, and will require the response of an application for an emergency protection order under the 'frustrated access' condition (see paragraphs 4.36 – 4.40 on section 44(1)(b)).

Prior investigations

4.11. An application by a local authority should always be preceded by an investigation under section 47 (see paragraphs 4.78 – 4.87 below). Since the order is for non-emergencies, there will be no justification for the investigation to be merely superficial. The court considering an application for a child assessment order will expect to be given details of the investigation and how it arose, including in particular details of the applicant's attempts to satisfy himself as to the welfare of the child by arrangement with the people caring for him (see also paragraph 4.23). If the court is not satisfied that all reasonable efforts were made to persuade them to co-operate and that these were resisted, the application is likely to founder on the third condition of section 43(1).

Commencement and duration

4.12. The court can allow up to 7 days for the assessment. The order must specify the date by which the assessment is to begin. The applicant should make the necessary arrangements in advance of the application, so that it would usually be possible to complete within such a period an initial multi-disciplinary assessment of the child's medical, intellectual, emotional, social and behavioural needs. This should be sufficient to establish whether the child is suffering, or likely to suffer, significant harm and, if so, what further action is required. Local authorities will need to review with the appropriate agencies in their area, the necessary procedures to be complied with to ensure that an assessment can be undertaken satisfactorily within the intentions and time limit of this part of the legislation. The applicant should be able to give details of the proposed arrangements to the court so that it may consider these when giving directions.

Effect of order

4.13. The child assessment order has two main effects. Firstly, it is a requirement that any person who is in a position to do so usually a person having parental responsibility for the child or having care of him at the time the order is made – produces him to the person named in the order so that the assessment may take place, and that he complies with any directions or other requirements included in the order. Secondly, it authorises the carrying out of the assessment in accordance with the terms of the order. Unlike the emergency protection order or interim or full care order, the holder of the order does not acquire parental responsibility for the child. A child of sufficient understanding to make an informed decision may refuse to consent to the assessment. The guardian *ad litem* may well be able to advise the court as to whether the child is of sufficient understanding to make such a decision. In performing this duty the guardian *ad litem* may need to seek the assistance of professionals in other disciplines, and particularly where a child suffers from a handicap which impairs his ability to communicate. The guardian *ad litem* will wish to explore with the child his or her reluctance to undertake an assessment, and advise the court accordingly. Providing the child with further advice may result in the child withdrawing his opposition, but all professionals should take particular care to avoid coercing the child into agreement even where there is a belief that the refusal to comply is itself the product of coercion by a parent, relative or friend.

Directions

4.14. The court should take advice from those presenting the case, and if necessary other professionals involved in the case (including the guardian *ad litem*) about what the assessment should cover, and may make directions accordingly (this may be based on information from any prior investigation under section 47). This may include, for example, whether it should be limited to a medical examination or cover other aspects of the child's health and development, and by whom and where it should be conducted. It may require that the child's usual doctor or another medical professional may participate and, for example, for the child's parents' medical representative to be present. The court may also make directions relating to the assessment of the child as seems appropriate and in the child's interest (section 43(6)(b)). The court should be asked to include in their order details of those to whom results of the assessment should be given.

Child away from home

4.15. Section 43(9) provides for keeping the child away from home for the purposes of the assessment. This is intended to be a reserve provision, and if used the number of overnight stays should be kept as low as possible. The assessment should be conducted with as little trauma for the child and parents as possible. It is important that the child assessment order is not regarded as a variant of the emergency protection order with its removal power: The purposes of the two orders are quite different. The child may only be kept away from home in the circumstances specified, namely:

(a) the court is satisfied that it is necessary for the purposes of the assessment;

(b) it is done in accordance with directions specified in the order; and it is limited to such period or periods (which need not be the full period of the order) specified in the order.

The need for an overnight stay might arise if the child were thought to have special needs or characteristics which necessitated overnight observation. It might be difficult to argue that an overnight stay "is necessary for the purposes of the assessment" simply because the arrangements made for the assessment would require him to travel very early or very late; the arrangements made by the applicant should aim to avoid difficulties of this kind. However, in exceptional circumstances, either for medical or social work reasons, an overnight stay might facilitate the completion of the assessment. Examples might include where the child has eating difficulties, seriously disturbed sleep patterns or other symptoms that would require 24 hour continuous observation and monitoring.

4.16. If the court directs that the child may be kept away from home, it must also give directions as it thinks fit about the contact the child must have with other persons during this period. A temporary overnight stay cannot be equated with being placed in care, but the court may well be guided on contact by the presumption of reasonable contact between a child in care and his parents, guardian and certain other persons established by section 34 (see paragraphs 3.76 – 3.86). It would also want to consider requests to be allowed contact from other persons who have to be notified of the hearing. The court may consider that the parents or other persons closely connected with the child should be allowed to stay with the child overnight, and the applicant for the order should consider offering this facility when asking for a direction that the child be kept away from home. As for all questions affecting the child that arise under the Act, the court must give paramount consideration to the child's welfare when considering contact and in doing so will wish to ascertain the views and feelings of the child. The guardian *ad litem* should also be able to assist in this respect.

Grounds for emergency protection order

4.17. The court is specifically required not to make a child assessment order if it is satisfied that there are grounds for making an emergency protection order and that it ought to make such an order instead of a child assessment order (section 43(4)). In that event, it may treat the application as an application for an emergency protection order and proceed under sections 44 and 45. The court may decide on hearing the evidence that the child's situation is more serious than the applicant judged, or new information indicating an emergency may emerge from the guardian *ad litem's* enquiries or other evidence. Although the different grounds and effect clearly distinguish the child assessment order for non-emergencies and the emergency protection order for emergencies, this power has been given to the court to guard against expressed fears that some applicants might opt for the less serious order when in reality the full powers of the emergency protection order are required. Local authorities and authorised persons should ensure that all staff concerned with investigations of this kind receive proper training in the correct use of these quite different orders and that applications for all court orders benefit from timely legal advice. The failure to act decisively due to an optimistic view of the impact of the child assessment order powers might in some circumstances have very serious consequences for the child concerned.

Other procedural requirements

4.18. Procedural requirements are outlined in section 43(11) and (12) and detailed more fully in the rules of court. They reflect the non-emergency nature of the order. The application should always be considered on notice at a full hearing in which the parties are able to participate. Therefore the application may be challenged at that stage. The rules of court provide for the circumstances in which and by whom an application to vary or discharge a child assessment order may be made. Again, unlike the emergency protection order, there is a right of appeal against the making, or the court's refusal to make, a child assessment order. Under section 91(14) and (15) the court may prevent a further application being made by particular persons (this includes a local authority) without the court's leave, or refuse to allow a further application for a child assessment order within six months without leave.

Failure to produce child

4.19. The applicant should be prepared for the possibility that the persons responsible for the child fail to produce him for the assessment in accordance with the order. Immediate enquiries should be made to establish whether there is an satisfactory explanation for non-production of the child. For example the child or the person caring for him may have been taken ill, or the requirements of the order may have been misunderstood. In circumstances like these, the person concerned should if possible be persuaded to comply immediately, otherwise the court should be asked to vary the terms of the order. Deliberate refusal to comply must add to concern for the child's welfare and would probably be sufficient to satisfy the significant harm or frustrated access conditions for an emergency protection order (see paragraphs 4.36 – 4.40 on section 44(1)(b)). If the developing circumstances make the case so urgent that there is no time to apply for an emergency protection order, the police should be asked to use their powers under section 46 to take the child into police protection. These can only be exercised, however, where access is not an obstacle and the police can in effect 'find' the child since there are no powers of search attached to section 46. In dire emergencies and for the purpose of saving life and limb, the police have reserve powers under the Police and Criminal Evidence Act 1984 to enter and search premises without a warrant. The potential significance of non-production for the child's welfare should not be underestimated; a person who had been abusing the child may be prepared to go to extreme lengths to prevent the child being seen or assessed. If the court considers when hearing the application for the child assessment order that there is a real danger that the order will not be complied with, it may, if the grounds for the greater order are satisfied, feel able to exercise its power to make an emergency protection order instead. Where there was insufficient information at an earlier stage to justify an application for an interim care or supervision order, non-production of the child for assessment would not be likely to add sufficiently to the evidence to make an application for either of those orders successful.

Child assessment orders and family proceedings

4.20. A child assessment order can subsist alongside a section 8 order or an education supervision order, but would not be required where a care order, emergency protection order or supervision order was in force. Under a care order, the authority would be able to arrange an assessment without specific court authority. If parents object the authority would have to use their powers under section 33(3)(b) to restrict the parents' exercise of their parental responsibility. Under a supervision order, the court could be asked to provide for an assessment in the order or give directions on the subject. Under an emergency protection order the court has specific direction powers concerning examination and assessment. Although the holder of the order has power to arrange examination to avoid disputes, in view of the short period during which the order has effect, the court should be asked to use their direction powers. In all these circumstances the child of sufficient understanding may refuse to submit to an examination or assessment.

Result of the Assessment

4.21. If the child is kept away from home for the purposes of the assessment and so serious a situation is revealed by the assessment that the child cannot be allowed to return home, an emergency protection order should be sought. Given the purpose of the child assessment order, it is anticipated that any follow-up will usually be through the provision of services for the child and the family. The authority (or authorised person) will need to consider what action to take in the light of the results of the assessment. Since it may not have been possible to conduct a comprehensive assessment within the period of the order, the findings may show that the child's health and development is being impaired but not identify the problem in full or be conclusive as to treatment.

4.22. The authority should consider whether further assessment is required and, if so, explore whether this can be arranged on a voluntary basis with the parents – who may have been persuaded by the child assessment order to be more positive – or should be pursued by way of an application for an interim care order or interim supervision order. The authority will have to consider whether the grounds for such an order would be satisfied. Where the initial assessment reveals a clear picture of the child's health and development and shows impairment which should not be ignored, the issue will be whether the child's welfare can be safeguarded and promoted by the provision of services under Part III (see Volume 2). Parents who are willing but may not be coping adequately may be helped by services of the kind to be provided for under paragraphs 4, 8 and 9 of schedule 2. Alternatively it might be best for the child to be provided with accommodation away from home for a period under section 20 while the parents are assisted.

Practice Issues

4.23. A number of important practice issues arise. One is that as far as possible the child assessment order should be used sparingly. Although a lesser order than others in Parts IV and V of the Act, it still represents substantial intervention in the upbringing of the child and could lead to yet further intervention. It should be contemplated only where there is reason for serious concern for the child. It should not be used for a child whose parents are reluctant to use the normal child health services. There should have been a substantial effort to persuade those caring for the child of the need for an assessment and to persuade them to agree to suitable arrangements voluntarily. When an assessment order is obtained it will be necessary for the parents to work with professional practitioners, and their co-operation during the process is essential if there is to be a useful assessment on which to base future action. The matter should be pursued on a multi-disciplinary basis (see paragraph 3.10), with pooling of information and consultation on handling the case. Any proposal to apply for a child assessment order and the arrangements to be discussed with the court for the assessment should be considered at a case conference convened under local child protection procedures. The authority will need to be sensitive to issues of gender, race and culture when formulating arrangements for an assessment. The parents may resist making the child available to local authority-appointed professionals but may be amenable to either the family doctor or an independent professional examining, or participating in the examination of the child. Arrangements of this kind may well provide sufficient information about the child's welfare and therefore should not be rejected by the local authority out of hand. If such arrangements were considered as satisfactory by the court hearing an application for a child assessment order this would provide the grounds for refusing the application. The emphasis on a multi-disciplinary assessment however suggests that the opinion of just one health professional will rarely be sufficient (see also the discussion in paragraphs 3.47 – 3.51).

4.24. Some parents, although willing to co-operate with the terms of a child assessment order, will have fears about the possible removal of their child as a result of the assessment. If used in the proper circumstances follow-up provision to a child assessment order will normally be by way of services to the child and his family to remedy any harm identified. The professional practitioner will need to make this clear and to stress the importance of encouraging the child's development with local authority support where necessary. There will, however, be cases where the results of the assessment dictate that the child should live away from home. The professional practitioner must not shirk from his responsibility in discussing this possibility and emphasising the benefits that will flow from the parents working in partnership with the local authority in these circumstances. Parents whose children have disabilities may be particularly worried by this kind of intervention and will require sensitive handling and reassurance that the intention is to enhance the life and abilities of their child, and that there is no intention to undermine their relationship with their child.

4.25. Although there may be occasions when the most obvious need is for a medical assessment, an assessment should always have a multi-disciplinary dimension. The difficulties and needs of the child must always be seen in the context of his social needs and the abilities and limitations of his parents, extended family and local community to meet these needs. All professional practitioners engaged in working with the family should be encouraged to contribute to a multi-disciplinary assessment both to pool information and to make proposals for future action to support the family.

4.26. A child assessment order puts the professional practitioners on notice and gives them up to seven days to conduct their assessment. This timescale was fixed with the intention of causing the least possible disruption to the child but allowing sufficient time for an assessment to produce the information required by professional workers and parents to formulate together plans for future action. In order to ensure that this work can be achieved within the timescale and that a detailed assessment programme can be presented to the court for it to be able to make the necessary directions, the professional team will need to plan in advance the matters to be covered during the assessment, the practical arrangements for doing this work, and the best way to involve parents and minimise trauma to the child. It has to be accepted that it may not always be possible within the seven days to do more than an initial assessment and obtain an indication of whether further work is necessary. Practitioners should consider ways of extending the assessment period on a voluntary basis if this becomes necessary. If the parents remain unco-operative and there is sufficient information to satisfy the grounds, an interim care or supervision order with conditions should be sought. (Where only one parent consents, no order would be required since section 2(7) empowers one parent to act alone. However, if one parent objects it would be necessary to obtain an order to avoid the possibility of private law proceedings under section 8 to resolve the dispute between the parents.)

4.27. Parents should always be told that a child assessment order may be applied for if they persist in refusing to co-operate, the reasons for making the application, the legal effect and detailed implications of the order, and the court procedure that would be followed. This information may be sufficient to persuade them that the authority are genuinely concerned about the child and that the parents should co-operate with the proposed voluntary arrangements. This information should be confirmed in writing backed up by easily understandable leaflets outlining local authority powers and duties and the rights and responsibilities of parents.

EMERGENCY PROTECTION ORDERS

Introduction

4.28. Emergency protection orders replace the much-criticised place of safety orders which could be obtained under a number of provisions in previous legislation. The purpose of the new order, as its name suggests, is to enable the child in a genuine emergency to be removed from where he is or be kept where he is, if and only if this is what is necessary to provide immediate short-term protection. Nearly every aspect of the new provisions, including the grounds for the order, its effect, opportunities for challenging it and duration, are different.

4.29. The essential features of the new provisions are:

(a) the court has to be satisfied that the child is likely to suffer significant harm or cannot be seen in circumstances where the child might be suffering significant harm;

(b) duration is limited to eight days with a possible extension of seven days;

(c) certain persons may apply to discharge the order (to be heard after 72 hours);

(d) the person obtaining the order has limited parental responsibility;

(e)   the court may make directions as to contact with the child and/or medical or psychiatric examination or assessment;

(f)   there is provision for a single justice to make an emergency protection order;

(g)   applications may be made in the absence of any other interested parties (ie *ex-parte*), and may, with the leave of the clerk of the court, be made orally;

(h)   the application must name the child, and where it does not, must describe him as clearly as possible.

4.30.   These key provisions have been limited to what is necessary to protect the child, but it remains an extremely serious step. It must not be regarded – as sometimes was the case with place of safety orders – as a routine response to allegations of child abuse or as a routine first step to initiating care proceedings. The new grounds require some evidence that the situation is sufficiently serious to justify such severe powers of intervention being made available. Nevertheless decisive action to protect the child is essential once it appears that the circumstances fall within one of the grounds in section 44(1). Under section 47(6) the authority must apply for an emergency protection order or another of the orders specified if they are refused access to the child or denied information about his whereabouts while carrying out enquiries, unless they are satisfied that the child's welfare can be satisfactorily safeguarded without their taking such action (see paragraph 4.85 below).

Removal of the alleged abuser

4.31.   Where the need for emergency action centres on alleged abuse of the child the local authority will always want to explore the possibility of providing services to and/or accommodation for the alleged abuser as an alternative to the removal of the child. This could be on a voluntary basis backed up by the provisions of schedule 2 paragraph 5 which gives authorities the discretion to provide assistance with finding alternative housing or cash assistance to the person who leaves the family home. Such practical assistance may be crucial in persuading the alleged abuser to co-operate in this way. Existing legislation makes no public law provision empowering a court to order an alleged abuser out of the family home. However, in certain circumstances private law remedies may be used to achieve the same effect, and the local authority should explore these where it is in the child's best interest to do so. The non-abusing parent may agree to apply to the county court for a short-term ouster injunction under section 1 of the Domestic Violence and Matrimonial Proceedings Act 1976 or to the magistrates' court for an exclusion order under section 16 of the Domestic Proceedings and Magistrates' Court Act 1978, forcing the alleged abuser out of the home. This may be particularly appropriate in sexual abuse cases where the non-abusing parent has no wish to protect or shield the alleged abuser and where immediate removal of the child is not always in the child's best interests.

Applications and Emergency Protection Order (Transfer of Responsibilities) Regulations

4.32.   Any person can apply to the court for an emergency protection order, as was the position in previous legislation for place of safety orders. Although in practice most applications are likely to be made by local authorities or 'authorised persons' it may sometimes be necessary in dire circumstances for a concerned relative or neighbour, say, to be able to act independently of the authorities in order to protect a child at risk. Rules of court will require the applicant to notify the local authority, amongst others, of the application, whereupon the authority's investigation duty under section 47 comes into play.

4.33.   The Regulations made under section 52(3) of the Act – the Emergency Protection Orders (Transfer of Responsibilities) Regulations 1991 – allow the authority to take over the order, and therefore the powers and responsibility for the child that go with it, if they consider that this course of action would be in the child's best interests. In forming their opinion Regulation 3 of these Regulations requires the authority to consult with the applicant of the emergency protection order and to consider the following factors:

(a) the ascertainable wishes and feelings of the child having regard to his age and understanding;

(b) the child's physical, emotional and educational needs for the duration of the emergency protection order;

(c) the likely effect on him of any change in his circumstances which may be caused by a transfer of responsibilities under the order;

(d) his age, sex and family background;

(e) the circumstances which gave rise to the application for the emergency protection order;

(f) any directions of the court and other orders made in respect of the child;

(g) the relationship (if any) of the applicant for the emergency protection order to the child; and

(h) any plans which the applicant may have in respect of the child.

The intention behind these Regulations is to ensure that in an emergency any individual can seek immediate and protective intervention and is not deterred or prevented from doing so by his inability to comply with any or all directions that the court may make. Applications by an authorised person (ie the NSPCC) are not exempt from these Regulations. It is however anticipated that the process of local dialogue and consultation between the NSPCC and the authority will mean that the transfer powers are rarely exercised without the latter's consent. The Regulations will not apply where the child who is subject to an emergency protection order is in a refuge in respect of which there is a Secretary of State's certificate under section 51.

Grounds for application

4.34. The court may only make an emergency protection order if it is satisfied that one of the grounds at section 44(1)(a), (b) or (c) is satisfied. As with the child assessment order, this condition is emphasised by the words "but only if" in the preamble to subsection (1). The applicant should not underestimate this point. In addition, section 1(1) and (5) apply (children's welfare in decision making by the court paramount, and presumption that no order unless making the order would be better than no order).

4.35. The three different grounds at section 44(1)(a), (b) and (c) deal with different situations. It is easiest to consider the grounds at section 44(1)(b) and (c) first. These are discussed below in paragraphs 4.36 – 4.40. The grounds at section 44(1)(a) are discussed at paragraph 4.41.

4.36. Section 44(1)(b) provides for an application by a local authority in particular circumstances – where, because they have reasonable cause to suspect that a child in their area is suffering, or is likely to suffer, significant harm, the authority is carrying out enquiries under section 47(1)(b) and those enquiries are being frustrated by access to the child being unreasonably refused, and they have reasonable cause to believe that access to the child is required as a matter of urgency. Although this ground applies only to a local authority, persons from other voluntary or statutory agencies may be acting on their behalf to undertake the enquiries.

4.37. The grounds at section 44(1)(c) provide for an application in the same circumstances by an authorised person (as defined by section 31(9)) who has been making enquiries except that they must also satisfy the court as to their reasonable cause for suspicion.

4.38. The circumstances in which these 'frustrated access' grounds are to be used must be distinguished from the child assessment order. They are for use in an emergency (where access is required as a matter of urgency) where enquiries cannot be completed because the child cannot be seen but there is enough cause to suspect the child is suffering or likely to suffer significant harm.

The child assessment order applies where there is a need for further investigation of the child's health and development but he is not thought to be in immediate danger.

4.39. The hypothesis of the grounds at section 44(1)(b) and (c) is that this combination of factors is evidence of an emergency or the likelihood of an emergency. The court will have to decide whether the refusal of access to the child was unreasonable in the circumstances. It might consider a refusal unreasonable if the person refusing had had explained to him the reason for the enquiries and the request for access, the request itself was reasonable, and he had failed to respond positively in some other suitable way – by arranging for the child to be seen immediately by his GP, for example. Refusal of a request to see a sleeping child in the middle of the night may not be unreasonable, but refusal to allow access at a reasonable time without good reason could well be. The parent who refuses immediate access but offers to take the child to a local clinic the following morning may not be making a reasonable refusal where the risk to the child is believed to be imminent or where previous voluntary arrangements have broken down. A person seeking access must produce evidence of his authority if asked to do so (section 44(3)) and failure to comply may well make a refusal to allow access reasonable. As a matter of good practice any professional practitioner seeking access to a child should show evidence of their authority whether asked to do so or not.

4.40. The local authority is required by section 47(6) to respond positively to a refusal of access or a denial of information about the child's whereabouts when they are conducting enquiries: they must apply for an emergency protection order or take other specified action unless satisfied that such action is unnecessary. These conditions for an emergency protection order reflect the importance of seeing the child when there are concerns about his welfare. The potential significance of unreasonable refusal of access for the child's welfare in suspicious circumstances is fully recognised in the grounds at section 44(1)(b) and (c), and there is now no justification for failing to act because of lack of information occasioned by inability to see the child. If the court makes an emergency protection order under condition (b) or (c), and it considers that adequate information as to the child's whereabouts is not available to the applicant but is available to someone else, such as the person who was last known to be looking after him, it can require that person in the order to disclose information about the child's whereabouts (section 48(1)). It can also authorise entry to premises to search for the child (section 48(3)) or other children (section 48(4)) (see paragraphs 4.52 – 4.57 below).

4.41. The other condition under which an emergency protection order may be made, at section 44(1)(a), is more of a general purpose provision for emergencies. For the criteria to be met the court must be satisfied that there is reasonable cause to believe that the child is likely to suffer significant harm:

(a) if he is not removed to accommodation provided by or on behalf of the applicant; or

(b) if he does not remain in the place in which he is then being accommodated (by implication, a safe place).

There is a clear distinction to be made in relation to the significant harm test in section 44(1)(a) as against subsections (b) and (c) discussed above. In the former it is the court that must have reasonable cause to believe; in the latter it is the applicant who must have reasonable cause to suspect.

4.42. The condition at section 44(1)(a) is for cases where the child has been seen, or seeing him may not be relevant, for example where a baby has just been born into a family with a long history of violent behaviour to young children. The authority may be carrying out enquiries under section 47 or in response to a direction under section 37, for example, and not have been refused access to the child. The test in relation to significant harm looks to the future. In other words, it may be necessary to remove him or keep him where he is in order to protect him from the likelihood of suffering significant harm. For the grounds under this subsection, past or present significant harm is relevant only to the extent that it indicates that he is likely to suffer significant harm in the near future. Unlike the requirement of previous legislation, there does not have to have been previous harm for the order to be made.

4.43. There are a number of additional points to be emphasised:

(a) in deciding whether to grant an emergency protection order on this ground the court will wish to know what it is that necessitates urgent action, whether, if removal of the child is necessary, it can be achieved with the co-operation of the parents and the provision of accommodation and whether a decision can wait until the parents have had an opportunity to properly prepare their case at an interim hearing. The applicant will be expected to give as much of this information as possible either orally or in the application form for the order. One of the reasons that this approach is necessary is because section 1(5) requires that the court should not make an order unless it would be better for the child to make the order than no order;

(b) the court may take account of any statement contained in any report made to the court in the course of, or in connection with, the hearing or any evidence given during the hearing which the court believes to be relevant to the applicant. This enables the court to give such weight as they think appropriate to any relevant hearsay, opinions, health visiting or social work records and medical reports (section 45(7)).

4.44. As with all orders under the Act, even where the above conditions apply the court will not automatically make an emergency protection order. It must still consider the welfare principle and the presumption of no order. In most cases it is unlikely that the parents will be present at the hearing. With only one side of the case before it the court will want to examine very carefully the information it is given, especially where the basis of the application is likelihood of future harm or inability to see the child. It may be that the initial order will be made for a very short time such as the next available hearing date so that an extension to the order will be on notice to parents and others.

Application procedure

4.45. Anyone can apply for an emergency protection order under section 44(1)(a) including a local authority or authorised person although, as mentioned above, subsections (b) and (c) are for applications by a local authority or authorised person respectively in particular circumstances. 'Anyone' could include a concerned relative or neighbour or teacher, and may include the police on behalf of the appropriate local authority, but the police should usually be able to use their powers under section 46 to take the child into police protection.

4.46. An emergency protection order will usually be heard *ex-parte* – that is, without other persons having to be given notice of the hearing and allowed to attend and make representations. Rules of court provide for applications to be heard *inter-partes* (at a full hearing with others who wish to attend able to do so) but the very fact that the situation is considered to be an emergency requiring immediate action will make this inappropriate or impracticable in most cases. However, if a court is available the application, including *ex-parte* applications, should be made to a court (as recommended by the report following the Cleveland Inquiry). It should be borne in mind that in certain instances to put the parents on notice of the application might place the child in greater danger.

4.47. Because of the emergency nature of the application and because most applications will be heard *ex-parte* rules of court require the applicant, rather than the court, to serve a copy of the application and the order within 48 hours on the parties to the proceedings, any person who is not a party but has actual care of the child and the local authority in whose area the child is normally resident if that authority is not the applicant. The need to inform parents of their rights and responsibilities under the new order is seen as crucial. Explanatory notes will be served with a copy of the order informing parents in easily understood language of what will happen to their child and what they can do next. These notes are printed on the back of the emergency protection order. The authority should consider making available similar written information in other languages where English is not the primary language of the families concerned.

Effects of an emergency protection order

4.48. While an emergency protection order is in force there are three effects. These are that a person who is in a position to do so must comply with any request to produce the child; the order authorises removal of the child or prevents his removal from where he is, and it gives parental responsibility to the applicant. However, the applicant can only do what is necessary to safeguard and promote the child's welfare in the exercise of his parental responsibility (section 44(5) and paragraph 4.58 below).

Directions as to disclosure of a child's whereabouts

4.49. In situations where persons looking after the child do not readily agree to hand the child over, the emergency protection order provides a formal direction to any person who is in a position to do so to comply with any request to produce the child to the applicant (section 44(4)(a)).

4.50. If the applicant for an emergency protection order does not know the whereabouts of a child, but that information seems to be available to another person, the court may order that person to disclose the information when requested to do so by the applicant (section 48(1)). This provision is intended to ensure that access to the child is not frustrated because information is being withheld from the applicant. The named person (or persons – the order may cite more than one person) will normally be the person who has previously refused to disclose the information to the applicant and who appears to the court to be in possession of the information, although the court may in theory name anyone. It would be advisable to ask courts as a matter of routine to attach this direction to an emergency protection order to avoid unnecessary returns to court in those cases where it is not known for sure that the child is at particular premises.

4.51. No one shall be excused from complying with a direction made under section 48(1) on the grounds that it may incriminate himself or his spouse, and "a statement or admission made in complying shall not be admissible in evidence against either of them for any offence other than perjury" (section 48(2)). This is intended to encourage witnesses to give evidence and provide vital information, and to avoid delay in children's cases. Failure to comply with the direction would be contempt of court.

Powers of entry

4.52. The Act gives the courts powers to authorise an applicant such as a social worker to enter and search premises for a child who is the subject of an emergency protection order (section 48(3)). Applicants should ask for this authority as a matter of course. This authorisation may be given when the court makes the order, and will specify which premises may be entered and searched, and by whom. The child will be the child named or described in the order. (see paragraphs 4.56 and 4.57 on supporting warrants.)

4.53. If the applicant believes there may be another child on the premises to be searched, who ought to be the subject of an emergency protection order, he should always seek an order authorising him to search for such a child (section 48(4)). Where the applicant cannot name the child, he should be described as clearly as possible in the order.

4.54. If on searching the premises the second child is found and the applicant believes that there are sufficient grounds for making an emergency protection order, the order authorising the search for the second child may be treated as an emergency protection order (section 48(5)). The authorised person must notify the court of the result of the search; ie, whether the child was found and if so what action was taken or is planned. The court should be told whether the authority to search for the child is now being treated as an emergency protection order. If so, and if the applicant for the order is not the local authority, the applicant will need to inform the authority accordingly so that they can fulfil their duty to investigate the child's circumstances under section 47. If the child is not found then the provisions of sections 49 and 50 apply, dealing with the abduction and recovery of children.

4.55. This provision is intended to cover the situation where the applicant believes there may be more than one child in the family or on the premises who is likely to suffer significant harm. In most cases the applicant will know if there are other children and should, if there are grounds, apply for an emergency protection order for each child. There may be occasions, however, when the applicant cannot identify the specific child but wants to check on the child or children in the same circumstances as the child for whom the emergency protection order is sought. Although an order under section 48(4) is quite distinct from an emergency protection order the need for it arises out of the same circumstances. It is for this reason and to avoid any unnecessary delay that an application for an order under section 48(4) has been incorporated in the application form for an emergency protection order so that where appropriate the two orders can be applied for and made simultaneously.

4.56. It is a criminal offence to intentionally obstruct an authorised person exercising his powers under section 48(3) and (4). If this does occur, or is anticipated, the court can issue a warrant authorising any constable to assist the authorised person in entering and searching the named premises (section 48(9)). The authorised person may accompany the police officer if he wishes, although the court may direct otherwise (section 48(10)(b)). In practice where it is the authority or NSPCC who is the applicant the social worker would normally accompany the police officer, as he will be responsible for the child when he has been removed from the premises, and it is desirable to reduce the number of officials who the child encounters in what will certainly be a very traumatic and difficult time. Any warrant which the court issues to the constable may direct that, if he chooses, the police officer may be accompanied by a doctor, nurse or health visitor (section 48(11)). It would be good practice always to request such a direction. The authorised person, if he is qualified to do so by virtue of his knowledge of the child, the family and the circumstances leading up to the application for the order, should advise the police whether such assistance would be desirable. A local authority will need to ensure that such a person is available if needed. The warrant will authorise the constable to use reasonable force if necessary in order to assist the applicant in the exercise of his powers to enter and search the premises for the child (section 48(9)).

4.57. When making an application for an emergency protection order, the applicant should consider whether at the same time he needs to apply for a warrant for a police officer to accompany him, if he is requesting authorisation to enter and search premises. This will of course depend upon the circumstances of the case, and the applicant's knowledge and previous experience of the people with whom he will be dealing. However, the emergency nature of the case should always be borne in mind; if any difficulties in gaining entry are foreseen, or if the applicant believes that he is likely to be threatened, intimidated or physically prevented from carrying out this part of the order, the possibility of simultaneously obtaining a warrant should always be considered. If necessary the advice of the local police should be sought when considering such an application. In dire emergencies the police can exercise their powers under section 17(1)(e) of the Police and Criminal Evidence Act 1984 to enter and search premises without a warrant for the purpose of saving life and limb. Similarly under section 25(3)(e) of the same Act the police may arrest without a warrant any person who has committed any offence where the arrest is necessary to protect the child from that person.

Removal of the child

4.58. The emergency protection order gives the applicant parental responsibility for the child but this is limited insofar as the applicant is authorised to exercise his powers to remove or prevent removal (from a safe place) only in order to safeguard and promote the welfare of the child. If an applicant gains access and finds the child is not harmed and is not likely to suffer significant harm he may not remove the child (section 44(5)). For example, if a suspected abuser vacates the child's home the holder of the emergency protection order would no longer be authorised to remove the child unless this was necessary to safeguard the welfare of the child. The power to do so would remain if the circumstances changed and the order was still in force. If removal is necessary the child is entitled to an explanation appropriate to his age and understanding of why he is being taken from his home and what will happen to him, even though as a party the older child or his solicitor or guardian *ad litem* will receive a copy of the application and order. A duty to explain to the child is laid on a police constable when taking a child into police protection (see paragraph 4.73).

Return of the child

4.59. When an emergency protection order is in force and the applicant has already removed the child, or prevented the child's removal from accommodation, the applicant is under a duty to return the child or, as the case may be, allow him to be removed if it appears to him that it is safe for the child to be returned or removed (section 44(10)). Where the applicant is satisfied that it is safe for the child to be returned, he is under a duty to return the child to the care of the person from whose care he was removed (section 44(11)(a)). If that is not reasonably practicable the applicant must instead return the child to the care of a parent of his, any person who is not a parent of his but has parental responsibility for him, or such person as the applicant considers appropriate. However, in this latter situation the agreement of the court must be sought (section 44(11)(b)).

4.60. If, after the child has been returned, there is again cause for concern the applicant may exercise his powers under the emergency protection order and remove the child once more, if it appears to him that a change in the child's circumstances makes it necessary to do so. This possibility should always be made clear to the parents where a child has been returned and the emergency protection order has not yet expired. In this situation the original duration of the emergency protection order is not extended and therefore the order would expire at the due date (section 44(12)). It is an offence to intentionally obstruct any person exercising his power (under section 44(4)(b)) to remove, or prevent the removal of a child.

Additional Directions

4.61. Where the court makes an emergency protection order it has the discretion to give additional directions as to the contact the child must be allowed to have with certain persons and may be allowed to have with any other named person (section 44(6)(a)). The court direction may impose conditions (section 44(8)). However subject to these, there is a general duty on the applicant under section 44(13) to allow the child reasonable contact with his parents, any person who is not a parent but has parental responsibility, any person with whom he was living before the order was made, any person in whose favour a contact order is in force with respect to the child (under section 8), any person who is allowed contact by virtue of an order under section 34 or anyone acting on behalf of any of these people. The court may give directions regarding contact not only when the emergency protection order is made, but also at any time while it is in force and the court may also vary the directions at any time (section 44(9)). The persons who are able to apply for a variation are prescribed by the rules of court.

4.62. It is anticipated that where the applicant is the local authority the court will leave contact to the discretion of the authority or order that reasonable contact be negotiated between the parties unless the issue is disputed, in which case specific directions can be sought at a hearing. In considering what is reasonable contact the authority will need to explore fully the wishes and feelings of the child. The authority may wish to limit contact or seek directions to control contact with families they believe to be troublesome and who are likely to upset the child or where there are allegations of sexual abuse and the contact needs to be supervised. In these circumstances, the authority should seek a direction defining contact. Where a direction has been made to define contact the authority will need to inform other agencies who may have regular dealings with the child, for example the school the child attends.

4.63. The court may also give directions about any medical or psychiatric examination or other assessment of the child (section 44(6)(b)) and may specify which types of examination or assessment should not be made unless the court directs otherwise (section 44(8)). In promoting the welfare of the child the court can therefore ensure that he is not subjected to unnecessary assessments. As a matter of good practice a local authority should always seek directions on assessment or examination of the child where this is likely to be an issue. Where possible it is anticipated that assessments will be undertaken by professionals agreed between the parties or arranged by the guardian *ad litem*. The court may direct, and the parents, if present, may request that the child's GP observe or participate in the assessment. Whether or not parents had an opportunity to challenge the making of a direction for a medical assessment they may wish to apply for it to be varied.

4.64. The court may give directions regarding medical or psychiatric or other assessment of the child not only when the emergency protection order is made, but also at any time while it is in force and the court may also vary the directions at any time. Where such directions are given, the child may, if he is of sufficient understanding to make an informed decision, refuse to submit to the examination or other assessment (section 44(7)). The consequences of such a refusal are discussed in paragraphs 3.50 and 3.51.

Duration

4.65. In the first instance an emergency protection order may be granted for up to 8 days (section 45(1)). However there are special provisions when the day on which the order would expire is a public holiday or a Sunday. In these situations if the 8th day of the order is a public holiday or Sunday the court may specify a period for the order which has the effect of extending it to noon on the first later day which is not such a holiday or a Sunday (section 45(2)). Where the child is in police protection and the designated officer applies for an emergency protection order the period of 8 days of any emergency protection order granted starts from the date that the child was taken into police protection and not from the date of the emergency protection order application (section 45(3)).

Extensions

4.66. The court may extend the period of the emergency protection order once only (section 45(6)) and for a period of up to seven days (including public holidays and Sundays). Rules of court require an application for an extension to be made on notice in a full *inter-partes* hearing by any person who has parental responsibility for the child as a result of an emergency protection order (ie, only a local authority or authorised person), and is entitled to apply for a care order with respect to the child (section 45(4)). However, the court may only extend the period of the order if it has reasonable cause to believe that the child concerned is likely to suffer significant harm if the order is not extended (section 45(5)). If there has been a genuine emergency and the authority believe care proceedings should follow it should normally be possible to proceed to satisfy the court as to the grounds for an interim order within the first period. If an extension is sought the court will want to be satisfied as to the reasons for the delay.

Appeals

4.67. There is no right of appeal against the making or refusal to make an emergency protection order, the extension of or refusal to extend an order, the discharge of or refusal to discharge an emergency protection order or the giving of or refusal to give directions in connection with an emergency protection order. However, despite the short duration of the order, there are opportunities available to challenge the making of an order and directions may be varied on application.

Discharges

4.68. No application for the discharge of an emergency protection order shall be heard by the court before the expiry of the period of 72 hours beginning with the making of the order. This will not prevent applications for discharge being made before 72 hours is up. A range of people may apply to the court for an emergency protection order to be discharged. These are; the child himself, a parent of his, any person who is not a parent but who has parental responsibility and any person with whom the child was living before the making of the order. However, an application to discharge an emergency protection order will not be allowed:

(a) where a person who would otherwise be entitled to apply for the emergency protection order to be discharged was given notice in accordance with rules of court of the hearing at which the order was made and was present at the hearing;

(b) where an emergency protection order has been extended in duration for a period not exceeding 7 days (section 45(11)). However, in this latter case the decision to extend the duration of the order can only be made at an *inter-partes* hearing so there would be an opportunity for representations to be made that there should be no extension.

4.69. The 72 hour provision will give parents and those listed in paragraph 4.68 an opportunity to clarify any confusion that may have arisen from the making of the order or any directions in their absence. It will also give them time to prepare their case should they wish to challenge the making of the order. It is not intended that 72 hours will become the effective time limit by which the authority must complete its assessment if it is to contest an application to discharge the order. The authority will be expected to go as far and as fast as is reasonably practical in undertaking the assessment. If an application comes to court for the discharge of an order after 72 hours and the assessment has not been completed the authority will advise the court accordingly and unless circumstances have so changed as to allay any concerns the authority may have had for the safety of the child it is unlikely that the court will agree to discharge the emergency protection order.

Child in refuge

4.70. Whilst a child is at a refuge, within the meaning of section 51, the organisation may apply for an emergency protection order under section 44(1) or ask the police to take the child into police protection under section 46. The grounds to be satisfied are that the organisation believes that the child is likely to suffer significant harm if he does not remain where he is, namely the refuge.

POLICE POWERS

Grounds and first steps

4.71. The police have important powers in protecting children under Part V of the Act. Where a constable has reasonable cause to believe that a child would otherwise be likely to suffer significant harm he may remove the child to suitable accommodation and keep him there. Alternatively, he may take such steps as are reasonable to ensure that the child's removal from hospital, or other place in which he is being accommodated, is prevented (section 46(1)). When a constable has exercised this power the child is referred to as having been taken into police protection (section 46(2)). This replaces a similar power in the Children and Young Persons Act 1969 which was used to hold children such as runaways and glue-sniffers or whose parents had abandoned them. It may also be used where a police officer attends a domestic dispute and finds a child living in unhygienic conditions. A child can only be taken into police protection once the police officer has found the child since there are no powers of search attached to this section of the Act. No child may be kept in police protection for more than 72 hours (section 46(6)).

4.72. As soon as is practicable after taking the child into police protection, the constable concerned has to ensure that the case is inquired into by the officer designated by the chief officer of the police area concerned. That officer, on completing the inquiry, has to release the child from police protection unless he considers that there is still reasonable cause for believing that the child would be likely to suffer significant harm if released (sections 46(3)(e) and (5)). What should be done in these circumstances is discussed below at paragraph 4.74.

Protection – responsibilities of constable

4.73. As soon as is reasonably practicable after the constable has taken a child into police protection there are a number of responsibilities which he must undertake which are different to the duties of the designated officer. These are to:

(a) inform the local authority within whose area the child was found of the steps that have been and are proposed to be taken with respect to the child (under section 46) and the reasons for taking them (section 46(3)(a));

(b) Give details to the local authority within whose area the child is ordinarily resident of the place at which the child is being accommodated (section 46(3)(b));

(c) Inform the child (if he seems capable of understanding) of the steps that have been taken, the reasons for taking them and of further steps that may be taken under this section (section 46(3)(c));

(d) Take such steps as are reasonably practicable to discover the wishes and feelings of the child (section 46(3)(d));

(e) Where the child was taken into police protection other than to accommodation provided on behalf of a local authority or to a refuge (see Volume 4), ensure that he is moved to such accommodation (section 46(3)(f));

(f) Take such steps as are reasonably practicable to give information to the child's parents, every other person who is not a parent of his but who has parental responsibility for him and any other person with whom the child was living immediately before being taken into police protection. The information to be given is, again, the steps that the constable has taken under section 46 with respect to the child, the reasons for taking them and the further steps that may be taken (under section 46) (section 46(4)).

Responsibilities of designated officer

4.74. The designated officer has a number of responsibilities in addition to inquiring into the case. He may apply on behalf of the local authority in whose area the child is ordinarily resident for an emergency protection order to be made in respect of the child. This application may be made whether or not the authority know of it or agree to it being made (section 46(7) and (8)). Good and effective channels of communication should mean that the police never make such an application without the local authority's knowledge and agreement. If they do so without local authority agreement protection can only extend for the duration of the order. The police cannot seek an extension to an emergency protection order nor can they commence care proceedings. The local authority where the child is ordinarily resident (and the local authority in whose area the child was found by the police if that is different) have the same duties to investigate and so ascertain whether they should take any action to safeguard or promote the child's welfare (section 47(1)) whether the child is in police protection or the subject of an emergency protection order. One such course of action is to ask the police to apply for an emergency protection order (section 47(3)(c)). In practice this means that the police and local authority will need to be in close liaison as soon as possible after the child has been taken into police protection

Parental responsibility

4.75. While a child is being kept in police protection neither the constable concerned nor the designated officer acquire parental responsibility. The designated officer must nevertheless do what is reasonable in all the circumstances to promote the child's welfare, bearing in mind the length of time police protection will last (section 46(9) – see also section 3(5)).

Contact with the child

4.76. The designated officer must also allow a range of persons to have contact with the child, as is in his opinion both reasonable and in the child's best interests. These are the child's parents, anyone else who has parental responsibility for him or with whom the child was living immediately before he was taken into police protection, a person who has in his favour an order relating to contact with the child or any person acting on behalf of any of the above. If the child in police protection is accommodated by the local authority for the area in which he usually lives, the authority is required to afford such contact to these people (section 46(11)). As with all sections of the Act relating to contact, the feelings and wishes of the child should be fully considered.

Inter-agency liaison

4.77. Local authorities will find it necessary to monitor and review at regular intervals their channels of communication with the police so that effective inter-agency working is achieved. Authorities will need to build on existing practice and guidelines developed under the aegis of the Area Child Protection Committee and the principles set out in 'Working Together'. This should ensure that no child taken into police protection need be accommodated in a police station , and that his reception into local authority accommodation is achieved with the minimum of trauma.

LOCAL AUTHORITY'S DUTY TO INVESTIGATE

4.78. A local authority is under a duty to investigate a child's welfare in a number of circumstances. Although the Act considers these after the relevant sections on the two principle new orders (the emergency protection order and the child assessment order), an application for either order should always be preceded by some kind of local authority investigation where the local authority is the applicant. Indeed the applicant is not likely to be able to satisfy the court of either set of grounds without being able to point to findings of an investigation, however limited this might be in some circumstances and especially in sudden emergencies. Action under section 47 (the local authority duty to investigate) should be seen as the usual first step when a question of child protection arises, and the guidance contained in the following paragraphs should therefore be read in conjunction with guidance on the protection orders.

Circumstances requiring investigation

4.79. A court in any family proceedings that comes before it has the power to direct the local authority to investigate a child's circumstances (section 37(1)). The local authority has a similar duty to investigate:

(a) when a court discharges an education supervision order and orders the local authority to investigate (paragraph 17(2) of schedule 3);

(b) where a local education authority notifies them that a child is persistently failing to comply with directions made under an education supervision order (paragraph 19 of schedule 3);

(c) where they are informed that a child who lives, or is found, in their area is the subject of an emergency protection order or is in police protection (section 47(1)(a));

(d) where the local authority have reasonable cause to suspect that a child who lives, or is found, in their area is suffering or is likely to suffer significant harm (section 47(1)(b)).

Focus of enquiries

4.80. Where a local authority have obtained an emergency protection order with respect to a child the authority must make (or have made on their behalf) the necessary enquiries to enable them to decide what action they should take to safeguard or promote the child's welfare (section 47(2)). In particular investigation must focus on whether the authority should make any application to the court or exercise any of their other powers under the Children Act with respect to the child (section 47(3((a)).

4.81. In the case of a child who is the subject of an emergency protection order and who is not in accommodation provided by or on behalf of the authority, the enquiries have to be directed towards establishing whether it would be in the child's best interests (while the emergency protection order remains in force) for him to be so accommodated (section 47(3)(b)).

4.82. In the case of a child who has been taken into police protection, the local authority's enquiries have to consider whether it would be in the child's best interests for the authority to ask for an application to be made by the police for an emergency protection order (sections 47(3)(c) and 46(7)).

4.83. In making their enquiries under section 47(1), the local authority must take such steps as are reasonably practicable (unless they are satisfied that they already have sufficient information) to obtain access to the child or to ensure that access to him is obtained on their behalf by a person authorised by them for the purpose. These enquiries should be made with a view to enabling the local authority to determine what action, if any, to take with respect to the child (section 47(4)).

Action following enquiries

4.84. Where, as a result of such enquiries, it appears to the authority that there are matters concerned with the child's education which should be investigated, they must consult the relevant education authority (section 47(5)). This may include such situations as the child's non-attendance at a named school, the fact that the child is not registered at any school, or where the school raises questions about the child's behaviour.

4.85. Where, in the course of making their enquiries the local authority or its representative is refused access to the child concerned, or information as to his whereabouts is denied, the authority must apply for an emergency protection order, a child assessment order, a care order or a supervision order, unless they are satisfied that the child's welfare can be satisfactorily safeguarded without an application (section 47(6)).

4.86. If, as a result of their enquiries under section 47, the authority decide not to apply for any of the above orders, they must consider whether it would be appropriate to review the case at a later date. If they decide that it would be appropriate the date on which that review is to begin must be set (section 47(7)). Where a local authority conclude that they should take action to safeguard or promote the child's welfare they shall take that action, so far as it is both within their power and reasonably practicable for them to do so (section 47(8)). As a matter of good practice, where action involves an application for an order and the application is refused, the authority should consider whether and when to review the case.

4.87. Where a local authority are conducting enquiries under section 47, it shall be the duty of any person specified (see below) to assist them with those enquiries, in particular by providing them with relevant information and advice, if called upon to do so. However, this provision does not oblige any person to assist a local authority where doing so would be unreasonable in all the circumstances of the case. What constitutes "unreasonable" will depend on local circumstances, and this will necessitate having good inter-agency liaison about what would normally be expected from co-operating authorities, and what could be done to resolve difficulties when they occur. The persons specified are any local authority, local education authority, local housing authority, health authority or NHS trust, and any person authorised by the Secretary of State (sections 47(9), (10) and (11)). Where appropriate the local authority will also wish to consult with other agencies including the police, probation service and local health authority, building on existing inter-agency networks and co-operation. Where a local authority are making enquiries under this section with respect to a child who appears to them to be ordinarily resident within the area of another authority, they must consult that other authority, who may undertake the necessary enquiries in their place (section 47(12)).

ABDUCTION OF CHILDREN IN CARE

4.88. A person shall be guilty of an offence if, knowingly and without lawful authority or reasonable excuse he takes the child away from any person who for the time being has care of him by virtue of a care order, emergency protection order or police protection. The offence extends to keeping such a person away from the 'responsible' person* or inducing, assisting or inciting such a child to run away or stay away from the responsible person (section 49(1)). The offence is restricted to a child who is in care, the subject of an emergency protection order or in police protection (section 49(2)).

4.89. Where a voluntary home, registered children's home or local authority or voluntary organisation foster parents provide a refuge for children who appear to be at risk of harm, and have been issued with a certificate by the Secretary of State under section 51, the organisation is exempt from the provisions of section 49 (see Volume 4).

RECOVERY ORDERS

4.90. A court may make a recovery order in respect of a child if there is reason to believe that the child has been unlawfully taken away or is being unlawfully kept away from the responsible person; the child has run away or is staying away from the responsible person; or the child is missing. Although the authority should promptly notify the police of all children looked after who abscond or are abducted, so that enquiries to trace the child may be instigated, the court's powers to make a recovery order are restricted to those children who are in care, are the subject of an emergency protection order or are in police protection (sections 50(2) and 49(2)).

4.91. The recovery order can only be made on the application of, and has to name, any person who has parental responsibility for the child by virtue of a care order, an emergency protection order or, where the child is in police protection, the designated officer (section 50(4)). It has also to name (or describe) the child. The application may be made *ex-parte*.

---

*The phrase 'responsible person' means any person who for the time being has care of the child by virtue of a care order, an emergency protection order or as a result of the police taking the child into police protection (sections 50(2) and 49(2)).

4.92. A recovery order can have four effects. These are:

(a) to direct any person who is in a position to do so to produce the child on request to any authorised person*;

(b) to allow a person authorised by the court to remove the child;

(c) to require any person who has information as to the child's whereabouts to disclose that information if asked to do so to a constable or officer of the court;

(d) to authorise a constable to enter any premises specified and search for the child, using reasonable force if necessary (section 50(3)). The premises may only be specified if it appears to the court that there are reasonable grounds for believing the child to be on them (section 50(6)).

4.93. Where a person is authorised he must, if asked to do so (and should, in any event), produce some duly authenticated document showing that he is authorised and that this is related to the identified recovery order. Obstructing a person exercising his power to remove a child is an offence (sections 50(9) and (10)). When an authorised person requires a person to disclose information about the whereabouts of the child, that person cannot be excused from complying with the request on the grounds that it might incriminate himself or his spouse of an offence (section 50(11)).

4.94. Where a child is made the subject of a recovery order whilst being looked after by a local authority, any reasonable expenses incurred by an authorised person in giving effect to the order should be recoverable from the authority. A recovery order made in England or Wales shall also have effect in Scotland as if it had been made there (sections 50(12) and (13)). A recovery order may also be made in Northern Ireland (section 50(14)).

---

*An 'authorised person' means any person specified by the court; any constable; any person who is authorised after the recovery order is made and by a person who has parental responsibility for the child by virtue of a care order or an emergency protection order to exercise any power under a recovery order. A 'designated officer' means an officer designated by the chief officer of the police areas concerned to secure that the case is inquired into following the remand of the child in an emergency into police protection (sections 50(7) and 46(3)(e)).

CHAPTER 5 <u>SECURE ACCOMMODATION</u>
<u>ORDERS</u>

5.1. Restricting the liberty of children is a serious step which must be taken only when there is no genuine alternative which would be appropriate. It must be a 'last resort' in the sense that all else must first have been comprehensively considered and rejected – never because no other placement was available at the relevant time, because of inadequacies in staffing, because the child is simply being a nuisance or runs away from his accommodation and is not likely to suffer significant harm in doing so, and never as a form of punishment. It is important, in considering the possibility of a secure placement, that there is a clear view of the aims and objectives of such a placement and that those providing the accommodation can fully meet those aims and objectives. Secure placements, once made, should be for only so long as is necessary and unavoidable.

5.2. Guidance in this chapter is confined to the basic requirements of section 25 and the associated Secure Accommodation Regulations. Further guidance and Regulations on wardship and the inherent jurisdiction of the High Court, good practice and case management of a child in a secure unit are contained in Volume 4 of the guidance.

CRITERIA FOR THE RESTRICTION OF LIBERTY

5.3. The use of secure accommodation by local authorities is subject to restrictions both in terms of the circumstances in which children they are looking after may be locked up and the maximum periods for which such accommodation may be used, with or without a court order. Similar restrictions are now also placed on children accommodated by health or local education authorities, or in residential care, nursing and mental nursing homes, unless such children are subject to detention under mental health legislation. (Section 25 and the Secure Accommodation Regulations 1991). Where such placements are to exceed 72 hours the local authority, or other body, must seek the authority of the court. The courts empowered to make secure orders are the juvenile, magistrates' or Crown Court in criminal proceedings (eg remands and committal for trial or sentence) and the family proceedings court (or county or High Court where a secure order is made in the course of other proceedings in such courts) in all other cases. Children in voluntary children's homes and registered children's homes may not be kept in secure accommodation.

5.4. Apart from certain juveniles remanded to local authority accommodation (see paragraph 5.3) no child described above may be placed, or kept, in accommodation provided for the purpose of restricting liberty unless it appears:

(a) that – (i) he has a history of absconding and is likely to abscond from any other description of accommodation; and

(ii) if he absconds, he is likely to suffer significant harm; or

(b) that if he is kept in any other description of accommodation he is likely to injure himself or other persons.

(section 25(1): for meaning of 'harm' and whether harm is 'significant' see sections 31(9) and 31(10) and the discussion in paragraph 3.19).

5.5. For certain children remanded to local authority accommodation, the criteria for restriction of liberty set out in paragraph 5.4 above are modified. The children are those:

"(i) charged with or convicted of an offence imprisonable, in the case of a person aged 21 or over, for 14 years or more; or

(ii) charged with or convicted of an offence of violence, or has been previously convicted of an offence of violence."

(Regulation 6(1)).

The modified criteria for restriction of liberty which apply in such cases are that such children may not be placed or kept in secure accommodation unless it appears that any accommodation other than that provided for the purpose of restricting liberty is inappropriate because:

"(a) the child is likely to abscond from such accommodation; or

(b) the child is likely to injure himself or other people if he is kept in any such accommodation."

(Regulation 6(2)).

APPLICATIONS TO THE COURT

5.6. A child meeting the above criteria may be placed in secure accommodation for a maximum period of 72 hours without court authority (Regulation 11(1), but see also Regulation 11(3) for exceptional arrangements at weekends and public holidays). A local authority, or other body, wishing to keep the child in secure accommodation beyond that period must make application to the relevant court for authority to keep the child in secure accommodation. Such applications may only be made by the local authority looking after the child or, as the case may be, the health authority, local education authority, or person carrying on the residential care home, nursing home or mental nursing home (Regulation 8).

Role of the court

5.7. It is the role of the court to safeguard the child's welfare from inappropriate or unnecessary use of secure accommodation, by both satisfying itself that those making the application have demonstrated that the statutory criteria in section 25(1) or Regulation 6, as appropriate, have been met and by having regard to the provisions and principles of section 1 of the Act. The court must therefore also be satisfied that the order will positively contribute to the child's welfare and must not make an order unless it considers that doing so would be better for the child than making no order at all. In non-criminal proceedings, applications to keep a child in secure accomodation are 'specified proceedings' within the meaning of section 41. The court is required to appoint a guardian *ad litem* for the child unless it is satisfied that it is not necessary to do so in the interests of the child.

Legal representation

5.8. A court must not exercise the powers conferred by section 25 unless the child who is the subject of the application is legally represented in that court. The only exception is where a child, having been informed of his right to apply for legal aid and having had the opportunity to do so, has refused or failed to apply (section 25(6)). The provision of legal aid in such proceedings is described in section 99 of the Act which, by amendment to section 15 of the Legal Aid Act 1988 requires that "representation must be granted where a child who is brought before a court under section 25 of the 1989 Act (use of accommodation for restricting liberty) is not, but wished to be, legally represented before the court."

Court powers

5.9. Where the court, having had regard to the provisions of section 1 of the Act, is satisfied that giving paramount consideration to the child's welfare requires the making of a secure order and that the relevant criteria for restriction of liberty have been met, it must make an order authorising the child to be kept in secure accommodation and specifying the maximum period the child may be so kept (section 25(4)).

5.10. For juveniles remanded to local authority accommodation the maximum period a court may authorise restriction of liberty is the period of the remand, except that no such order may extend beyond a period of 28 days (Regulation 14). Other than when the child is committed to a Crown Court for trial, when different remand arrangements apply, the maximum period will be the period of remand and authority to keep a child in secure accommodation will need to be renewed (if application is made by the local authority) on each occasion the child returns to court for his remand case to be reviewed. In Crown Court cases the secure order may not extend beyond 28 days and a further application must be made by the local authority accommodating the child if they wish to keep the child in secure accommodation beyond that period.

5.11. For non-remand cases the maximum periods a court may authorise a child to be kept in secure accommodation are:

(a) three months, on first application to the court (Regulation 12); or

(b) six months, in respect of any further application to the court to continue to keep that child in secure accommodation (Regulation 13).

5.12. On any adjournment of the hearing of an application for authority to keep a child in secure accommodation, the court may make an interim order permitting the child to be kept during the period of adjournment in secure accommodation (section 25(5)).

Appeals

5.13. The arrangements for appeals against the granting, or otherwise, of authority to keep a child in secure accommodation are set out in section 94 of the Act. Both the child and the authority, or body, making application to the court may appeal to the High Court against the making, or refusal to make, by a magistrates' court an order under section 25.

CHAPTER 6 — JUVENILE OFFENDING AND THE CHILDREN ACT

JUVENILE OFFENDING AND THE CHILDREN ACT

INTRODUCTION

6.1. The Children Act contains certain provisions relating to juveniles who are at risk of committing offences or who have been accused or convicted of a criminal offence. The most far-reaching are:

(a) the new duty laid on local authorities to encourage juveniles within their area not to commit offences;

(b) the new duty laid on local authorities to take reasonable steps designed to reduce the need to bring criminal proceedings against juveniles in their area;

(c) the abolition of the criminal care order;

(d) the new power given to courts to attach residence requirements to criminal supervision orders.

These, and the other criminal implications of the Children Act, are set out below.

PREVENTION OF CRIME AND DIVERSION FROM PROSECUTION

6.2. Paragraph 7 of schedule 2 of the Act stipulates that every local authority shall take reasonable steps designed (*inter alia*):

(a) to encourage juveniles within its area not to commit offences; and

(b) to reduce the need to bring criminal proceedings against juveniles within its area.

These duties lay an obligation on each local authority to prevent juvenile crime and to contribute to local arrangements for diverting juvenile offenders from criminal proceedings. (These duties are laid on local authorities as a whole, but in practice the social service department is likely to assume the lead responsibility within a local authority).

6.3. Local authorities will need to consider how to carry out these specific duties when exercising their powers under the Children Act generally; and they will need to discharge them in co-operation with other agencies concerned with juvenile offenders (see paragraphs 6.6 and 6.9 below). These duties do not, however, lay the principal responsibility for dealing with juvenile offenders on local authorities – this remains with the police. Nor is it expected that local authorities or other agencies will be able to prevent juvenile crime altogether.

6.4. The services that local authorities can make available include:

(a) the provision of advice and support to parents, given the role of parents in discouraging offending;

(b) 'preventative' intermediate treatments for young people at risk of offending;

(c) supervision for juvenile offenders (where authorised by a court), with or without intensive intermediate treatment;

(d) the general provision of youth and community services.

6.5. To comply with their new duties, local authorities will need to review the range of facilities that already exists for juveniles and their families. In doing so they will need to collect information such as local patterns of juvenile crime and numbers of arrested juveniles in order to identify gaps in services and how they might best be filled. They will also need to collect data on the gender and ethnicity of juvenile offenders; this will enable them to monitor the local juvenile justice system to see if a juvenile's gender or ethnic background affects the way in which the judicial system deals with him or her.

6.6. To this end, each local authority will need to liaise closely, at a senior level, with other agencies concerned with juvenile offenders and young people at risk of offending, e.g. the police, magistrates, probation service, schools and youth and community services. Voluntary organisations and local community leaders will also have an important role in helping to devise a local juvenile crime prevention strategy for each area. Steps should be taken to establish a standing committee, representing the relevant agencies, to formulate the strategy and keep it under review. This standing committee could usefully be the general crime prevention group whose establishment in each area was recommended in the inter-departmental circular LAC(90)5 (see paragraph 6.7 below). It should be noted that it is vital for one member of the standing committee to take the lead role in promoting liaison between all the agencies represented on the committee. However, it is not necessary for this role to be filled by the local authority representative; it can equally well be filled by the representative of another statutory agency or by a representative of the voluntary sector or the local community.

6.7. Local authorities will wish to note that advice on juvenile crime prevention is contained in an inter-departmental circular LAC(90)5, "Crime Prevention – the Success of the Partnership Approach", and in the booklet enclosed with the circular. This advice stresses the importance of an inter-agency approach to crime prevention. It will be of use to local authorities in helping them to set up strategies to encourage juveniles within their areas "not to commit offences". The main features of this guidance are:

(a) the importance of establishing an inter-agency crime prevention committee;

(b) the role that can be played in this committee by community leaders and representatives of the voluntary sector;

(c) the need for this committee to draw up a strategy for crime prevention that is flexible enough to allow a response to crime at all levels, from street to county;

(d) the designation of an individual or agency of the committee (not necessarily police or social services) to co-ordinate the efforts of all members of the committee and the agencies they represent;

(e) the importance of obtaining information on the number and pattern of offenders and offences (see also paragraph 6.5 above), in order to identify the appropriate action;

(f) the help that the media can give in helping to publicise local crime prevention initiatives;

(g) the need to ensure that crime prevention committees, once set up, continue in existence;

(h) the need to identify sources of funding for this work, which need not be from public money (e.g. businesses and community organisations may provide money for the improvement of their surroundings).

6.8. The circular identifies crime prevention work as developing from this base in four broad ways:

(a) by improving the quality of work in the field and increasing the effectiveness of initiatives aimed at crime and the fear of crime;

(b) by stimulating activity in places and in fields where it has yet to develop;

(c) by improving the quality of local information on which crime prevention work is based, dealing with it in a more sophisticated way, and developing communication with the public about local responses to crime; and

(d) by developing strong local organisational support for clearly defined work.

6.9. Attention is also drawn to Home Office circular 59/1990, "The Cautioning of Offenders", which stresses the importance of inter-agency participation in relation to the cautioning of offenders. This circular makes the following points about the use of cautions:

(a) police forces may well find it useful to discuss cautioning strategies and objectives, especially in relation to juvenile offenders, with other agencies such as the probation service, social services departments and the Crown Prosecution Service;

(b) such discussions should take place at senior officer level;

(c) in making individual cautioning decisions about juveniles, the police should invite juvenile liaison panels to review any case where the decision whether or not to caution a juvenile is in doubt. (Juvenile liaison panels are normally based around police, probation service, education service and social services representatives);

(d) It will be useful, in certain cases, if the cautioned person who has particular problems can be referred – on a voluntary basis – to other agencies which can provide guidance, support and involvement in the community. This help might involve (*inter alia*) help with accommodation and or benefits; basic education; pre-employment training; out of school and leisure time activities; and help from alcohol or drugs projects;

(e) the purpose of the caution is to deal quickly with a minor offender, to divert him from the courts and to lessen the chances of him re-offending;

(f) offenders may be cautioned more than once; the nature of the offender and the offences will affect any decision as to whether this happens;

(g) at the same time, cautioning is not to be used inappropriately, e.g. in response to a very serious offence.

Local authorities, and other agencies concerned with juvenile offenders, will need to bear in mind the advice contained in this circular when discussing with the police both local cautioning strategy and objectives and – where this is necessary – individual cases where a caution is being considered.

CARE, SUPERVISION AND OTHER ORDERS MADE IN CARE PROCEEDINGS: ABOLITION OF 'OFFENCE' CONDITION

6.10. Section 1(2)(f) of the Children and Young Persons Act 1969 lists the commission of a criminal offence as one of the criteria whereby various orders may be made in care proceedings. However, section 90(1) of the Children Act abolishes the power of a court to make an order in care proceedings as a result of the fulfilment of this 'offence' condition. Sections 31 to 35 and Parts I and II of schedule 3 of the Children Act make new provision for civil care and supervision orders.

Transitional arrangements

6.11. The Annex to this Volume provides guidance on:

(a) orders made under section 1 of the Children and Young Persons Act 1969;

(b) care orders made under section 15 of the Children and Young Persons Act 1969 upon the discharge of supervision orders made under section 1 of that Act; and

(c) supervision orders made under section 21 of the Children and Young Persons Act 1969 upon discharge of care orders made under section 1 of that Act.

The transitional arrangements apply to all the above orders, including those made following the fulfilment of the 'offence' condition.

CARE ORDERS IN CRIMINAL PROCEEDINGS: ABOLITION

6.12. Section 90(2) of the Children Act abolishes the power of a court to make the following orders (referred to as "criminal care orders"):

(a) a care order in criminal proceedings made under section 7(7)(a) of the Children and Young Persons Act 1969;

(b) a care order made under section 15(1) of the Children and Young Persons Act 1969 upon discharge of a supervision order made in criminal proceedings under section 7(7)(b) of the same Act.

Transitional arrangements

6.13. The transitional arrangements are set out in paragraph 36 of schedule 14 to the Children Act. If a juvenile is subject to a criminal care order when section 90(2) of the Act comes into force, the order will continue to have effect until the end of the period of six months beginning the day that section comes into force, unless it is brought to an end before then.

6.14. While the criminal care order remains in force, any relevant provisions of the Children and Young Persons Act 1969 and the Child Care Act 1980 shall continue to apply to it as if the provisions repealed remained in force. Under these, the care order may be brought to an end before the six month period has expired.

6.15. Furthermore, while the criminal care order remains in force, a court may, on the application of the 'appropriate person' (see paragraph 6.16 below) discharge it and replace it with one of the following:

(a) a residence order (section 8 of the Children Act);

(b) an education supervision order (section 36 of the Children Act) (regardless of section 36(6) which normally prevents such an order being made in respect of a child in local authority care);

(c) a criminal supervision order with a residence requirement (section 90(3) and paragraph 23 of schedule 12 of the Children Act). Such an order, when made under these provisions, may stipulate a period of residence in local authority accommodation for no more than six months. It may also stipulate that, during the period of the residence requirement, the juvenile shall not live with a named person (see also paragraphs 6.20-6.30 below).

Definition of 'appropriate person'

6.16. The 'appropriate person' mentioned in paragraph 6.15 is:

(a) for a section 8 residence order: Anyone (other than the local authority) who has the leave of the court;

(b) for a section 36 education supervision order: The local education authority;

(c) for a care or supervision order in care proceedings (section 31) or a criminal supervision order with a residence requirement (paragraphs 36(5) and (6) of schedule 14): The local authority to whose care the juvenile was committed by the original criminal care order.

SUPERVISION ORDERS IN CRIMINAL PROCEEDINGS

6.17. Supervision orders in criminal proceedings ('criminal supervision orders') consist of:

(a) criminal supervision orders made under section 7(7)(b) of the Children and Young Persons Act 1969; and

(b) criminal supervision orders made under section 21(2) of the Children and Young Persons Act 1969 upon the discharge of criminal care orders made under section 7(7)(a) of the same Act.

The status of any criminal supervision orders current when the Children Act comes into force will not be affected by the Act (section 35 and Parts I and II of schedule 3 of the Children Act refer only to supervision orders made in care proceedings). Consequently the Act contains no transitional arrangements for such orders.

6.18. The Act does, however, repeal section 21 of the Children and Young Persons Act 1969. Consequently, after a date to be specified courts will not be able to make criminal supervision orders under section 21(2) of the Children and Young Persons Act 1969 on the discharge of a criminal care order. Any such orders current when the Children Act is brought into force will continue until terminated by the existing arrangements under the Children and Young Persons Act 1969.

6.19. Courts will continue to be able to make criminal supervision orders under section 7(7)(b) of the Children and Young Persons Act 1969. The Children Act amends the powers of courts to include requirements in such orders and these amendments are set out in detail in paragraphs 23 and 24 of schedule 12 to the Act.

6.20. Paragraph 23 of of schedule 12 inserts a new section 12AA into the Children and Young Persons Act 1969. (The existing sections 12 – 12D were inserted into the Children and Young Persons Act 1969 by Part I of schedule 10 to the Criminal Justice Act 1988.) The new section 12AA gives the court making a criminal supervision order the power to attach a 'residence requirement' to it requiring the juvenile to live for a specified period of time in local authority accommodation. (This requirement should not be confused with the residence order that can be made in civil proceedings under section 8 of the Children Act.)

The residence requirement

6.21. The purpose of the residence requirement is not punitive; it is designed to help a young person to work through his problems. A young person's circumstances may contribute to his offending: For example, he may be living rough and stealing to survive; he may have experienced a lack of parental control; or his life at home may be unsatisfactory in other respects. The residence requirement is designed to remove such a young person from the surroundings that are contributing to his offending behaviour, and to place him in local authority accommodation while the local authority enables him to work through the problems associated with his home surroundings. The aim must be to assist the young person to deal with his problems, and to stop him re-offending, even when he does return to his home surroundings. It therefore follows that the role of the social workers responsible for him must be to care for and assist him, and not simply to act as warders.

6.22. The period of time spent in local authority accommodation under the residence requirement will be decided by the court, but may be a period of up to six months. The residence requirement may also specify that the juvenile is not to live with a named person or persons, although it cannot specify where the juvenile is to be accommodated. If the "named persons" are the juvenile's family, it will still be necessary to ensure that contact between the juvenile and his family is maintained. It will also be necessary to ensure the continuity of the juvenile's education.

6.23. The residence requirement must designate the local authority that is to receive the juvenile, and that local authority must be the authority in whose area the juvenile resides. The court must consult the local authority before imposing a residence requirement. When consulted, the local authority will wish to give its views on the suitability of such a requirement in the light of any knowledge it may have of the juvenile (see also paragraphs 6.25 and 6.26). It will also wish to explain to the court what resources are available to implement a residence requirement, e.g. short-term foster placements, and places in community homes.

6.24. The court may only impose a residence requirement if the following conditions are all met:

(a) a criminal supervision order has previously been made in respect of the juvenile;

(b) that order imposed *either*:

    (i) a requirement under section 12A(3) of the Children and Young Persons Act 1969 (e.g. to take part in a programme of intermediate treatment);

    or

    (ii) a residence requirement;

(c) the juvenile is convicted of an offence which:

    (i) was committed while that order was in force;

    (ii) if it had been committed by a person over the age of 21 would have been punishable with imprisonment; and

    (iii) in the opinion of the court is serious;

(d) the court is satisfied that the behaviour that constituted the offence was due, to a significant extent, to the circumstances in which the juvenile was living. However, this condition does not apply if condition (b)(ii) is met.

6.25. Unless condition (b)(ii) applies, a court must obtain a social enquiry report to enable it to satisfy itself that the condition has been met. The social enquiry report will have to be provided by either by the probation service or by the social services department, and in each local authority area these two agencies will need to agree on the division between them of the responsibility for providing such reports. If the probation service provides the social enquiry report it should consult the social services department before recommending the imposition of a residence requirement, since the requirement imposes duties on the social services department. (However, the views of the social services department are not, of course, binding on the probation officer preparing the report.)

6.26. The social enquiry report must make particular reference to the circumstances in which the juvenile was living. This places on the writer of the report a responsibility to undertake a full assessment of the juvenile's home or other circumstances in which he has been living. It will not be enough to make a general comment on the family or other circumstances. Any cause and effect between the juvenile's circumstances and his offending must be based on clear, demonstrable evidence. Further assessment will be required about the extent to which the juvenile's circumstances are a significant factor in his offending when set against other factors. It should be borne in mind that one of the primary objectives of a residence requirement is to provide an opportunity for both the juvenile and his family or other carers to address the specific difficulties which give rise to his offending. Any assessment, therefore, that concludes that there is a significant link between the juvenile's current living circumstances and his offences should be accompanied by a clear action plan about the work to be done to resolve the difficulties.

6.27. The requirement at paragraph 6.25 does not apply if the court has already before it a social enquiry report containing sufficient information about the circumstances in which the juvenile is living.

6.28. A court may not impose a residence requirement on a juvenile who is not legally represented in court when the court is deciding whether to impose the requirement, unless:

(a) the juvenile has applied for legal aid for the proceedings and the application was refused on the grounds that it did not appear that his resources were such that he needed assistance; or

(b) he has been informed of his right to apply for legal aid for the proceedings and has had the opportunity of doing so, but has refused or failed to apply.

If a juvenile does choose not to be legally represented in court, it is most important that the social services department help him to understand the implications of refusing to be represented.

6.29. A supervision order imposing a residence requirement may also impose any of the requirements mentioned in sections 12, 12A, 12B and 12C of the Children and Young Persons Act 1969.

6.30. The Regulations governing the review of children's cases will apply to juveniles subject to a residence requirement. Reference should be made to Volume 3, which contains guidance on reviews of cases and arrangements for placement of children. Reference should also be made to the duty of local authorities to receive, and provide accommodation for, juveniles who are the subject of a supervision order with a residence requirement attached (section 21(2)(c) of the Children Act). The existence of this last duty, under section 21 of the Act, means that other local authority duties under Part III of the Act generally apply to juveniles made subject to a residence requirement. The other duties may include the duties and powers of local authorities under section 24 of the Act to prepare young people for leaving care and to provide aftercare where appropriate. (See also paragraph 6.43).

6.31. Local authorities will also wish to note that paragraph 24 of schedule 12 to the Children Act makes certain consequential amendments by inserting references to section 12AA of the Children and Young Persons Act 1969, where appropriate, in section 15 of the same Act (variation and discharge of supervision orders).

CIVIL AND CRIMINAL ORDERS

6.32. Section 31(7) of the Children Act stipulates that a court may not consider any application from any authorised person (NSPCC) to make a care order or a supervision order in care proceedings if the juvenile concerned is already subject to (*inter alia*) a care order, a civil supervision order or a criminal supervision order under section 7(7)(b) of the Children and Young Persons Act 1969. This stipulation does not, however, apply to any application made by a local authority.

'RECOGNISANCE' ORDERS IN CRIMINAL PROCEEDINGS

6.33. Under section 7(7)(c) of the Children and Young Persons Act 1969, a court, upon convicting a juvenile offender, has power "with the consent of (the offender's) parent or guardian, to order the parent or guardian to enter into a recognisance to take proper care of him and exercise proper control over him".

6.34. Section 2(13) of the Children and Young Persons Act 1969 imposed limits on the amount and period of any such recognisance. The whole of section 2 of the Children and Young Persons Act 1969 is repealed by the Children Act. However, section 2(13) of the Children and Young Persons Act 1969 has been re-enacted without change by the new sections 7(7B) and 7(7C) of the Children and Young Persons Act 1969 as inserted by the Children Act (see paragraph 21 of schedule 12 to the Children Act). Under the new provisions a recognisance may not exceed £1,000.

REMANDS

6.35. Paragraph 26 of schedule 12 to the Children Act inserts a new section 23 into the Children and Young Persons Act 1969. This replaces former section 23 of the Children and Young Persons Act 1969 (remands to local authority accommodation). The provisions of the former section 69 of the Children Act 1975 (unruliness certificates) are also now brought within the new section 23.

6.36. The only variation from the existing law is that juveniles are no longer remanded to "the care of a local authority" but to "local authority accommodation" (section 23 of the Children and Young Persons Act 1969 as amended by the Children Act 1989). As such, they become children 'looked after' by a local authority within the meaning of Part III of the Act (section 22(1)). Parental responsibility remains with the child's parents. However, in considering how they exercise their general powers in relation to such children under section 22, local authorities may have regard to the need to protect members of the public from serious injury (section 22(6)). Because of the transitory nature and status of remanded alleged juvenile offenders it is not practicable to make long-term plans for such children, but interim contingency plans might be formulated to take account of the sentencing options available to the court if convicted.

6.37.   While a remand to 'local authority accommodation' continues to leave the authority with discretion about the most appropriate placement for a juvenile on remand, full account should be taken of the fact that:

(a) the court has already been required to consider why the juvenile should not be bailed and allowed to return home, and has determined that this would not be appropriate;

(b) the local authority has a responsibility to ensure that the juvenile is produced in court at the date, place and time specified, and to take all reasonable steps to protect the public from the risk of the juvenile committing further offences during the remand period. (The nature of the steps required to protect the public will depend on the juvenile concerned and on the alleged offence).

6.38. It is important that a comprehensive range of services and facilities are available locally for remanded juveniles to ensure that they are not remanded to a penal establishment on a certificate of unruliness or placed in a secure unit unless it is absolutely necessary. To this end, local authorities may find it useful to develop bail support schemes and other supportive services in the community. In addition, many local authorities have found it useful to develop services within the childcare system for remanded juveniles, e.g. remand fostering schemes and residential accommodation with very high levels of staff supervision. Local authorities will also wish to note the role that the voluntary sector can play in providing a range of services for remanded juveniles.

6.39. On each occasion that a juvenile is returned to the court for the remand to be reviewed, careful consideration should be given to advising the court whether alternative arrangements might be considered. For example, where a juvenile has been remanded to a penal establishment on a certificate of unruliness, the court may be willing to consider a remand to local authority accommodation if they are presented with a clear statement of how the juvenile would be accommodated within the child care system in such a way that the public would be protected from the risk of further offending and that he would be produced in court when required. Similarly, where a juvenile has been remanded to local authority accommodation, the court may be prepared to grant bail if it can be demonstrated that an effective package of support in the community can be provided.

PROVISION OF ACCOMMODATION BY LOCAL AUTHORITIES

6.40. Section 21 of the Children Act sets out certain categories of child for whom local authorities must provide accommodation. These include:

(a) Juveniles whom local authorities are requested to receive under section 38(6) of the Police and Criminal Evidence Act 1984. (ie those arrested by the police, who have not yet appeared in court and who are to be provided with local authority accommodation until they make such an appearance - see also paragraph 53 of schedule 13 to the Children Act.) In determining how such juveniles are to be accommodated, the authority will need to have regard to the fact that the police custody officer has not ordered the juvenile's release from police detention, either on bail or without bail, under section 38(1) of the Police and Criminal Evidence Act 1984;

(b) Juveniles on remand under the revised section 23(1) of the Children and Young Persons Act 1969 (although this does not affect an authority's discretion to make such placement as it considers appropriate);

(c) Juveniles subject to a supervision order with residence requirement under section 12AA of the the Children and Young Persons Act 1969 (see paragraph 6.20 above).

(see paragraph 6.20 above)

Absconding from accommodation

6.41. Paragraph 27 of schedule 12 to the Children Act substitutes a new section 32(1A) of the the Children and Young Persons Act 1969. This section now permits the arrest, without warrant, of any juvenile who is absent without permission from:

(a) A place of safety to which he has been taken under section 16(3) of the Children and Young Persons Act 1969 (arrest of a supervised person to ensure his attendance at court);

(b) Local authority accommodation in which he is required to live under a residence requirement attached to a supervision order (section 12AA of the the Children and Young Persons Act 1969);

(c) Local authority accommodation to which he has been remanded under section 23(1) of the the Children and Young Persons Act 1969.

Local authorities should issue clear guidelines to their staff on the circumstances in which the police should be notified that a juvenile is absent without permission. They should take into account the fact that juveniles may return late from a permitted absence.

6.42. A juvenile so arrested may be conducted to the place of safety, the local authority accommodation or "such other place as the responsible person may direct"; and in each case, at the expense of the 'responsible person'. The 'responsible person' is defined as:

(a) section 16(3) cases: "The person who made the arrangements under section 16(3)" of the Children and Young Persons Act 1969;

(b) section 12AA cases and section 23(1) cases: The local authority concerned.

MISCELLANEOUS

Advice and assistance

6.43. Section 24 of the Children Act sets out extended and simplified local authority powers and duties to:

(a) prepare children whom they are looking after for the time when they cease to be so looked after; and

(b) provide financial and other assistance, when needed, to children who have ceased to be looked after by the local authority.

Detailed guidance on these powers and duties is given in the chapters on aftercare in Volumes 3 and 4 in this series of guidance. However, local authorities will wish to note that these powers and duties extend to the following children:

(i) those detained under section 38(6) of the Police and Criminal Evidence Act 1984;

(ii) those remanded to local authority accommodation under section 23 of the Children and Young Persons Act 1969, as amended by the Children Act;

(iii) those subject to a care order made under section 1 or section 15 of the Children and Young Persons Act 1969 (whether or not the 'offence condition' was satisfied) when the Children Act comes into force;

(iv) those subject to a care order under section 7(7)(a) of the Children and Young Persons Act 1969 immediately before the Children Act comes into force;

(v) those subject to a supervision order made under section 7(7)(b) of the Children and Young Persons Act 1969 with a residence requirement attached under section 12AA of the same Act;

(vi) those detained under section 53 of the Children and Young Persons Act 1933, following the commission of a grave crime, if they are looked after in local authority accommodation.

These powers and duties will apply if the child ceases to be looked after by the local authority after reaching his 16th birthday and if the other conditions set out in section 24 of the Act are satisfied. The provisions can apply until the child reaches his 21st birthday. the powers and duties will be exercised by the local authority in whose area the juvenile proposes to live after leaving any of the above forms of accommodation.

Courts arrangements

6.44. Local authorities will wish to note that under the Children Act the juvenile courts will continue to hear criminal proceedings affecting juveniles. Civil proceedings affecting juveniles, if heard by magistrates, will become the responsibility of the domestic courts, which will be known as family proceedings courts (section 92(1) of the Children Act).

Criminal Justice Bill

6.45. The criminal justice white paper "Crime, Justice and Protecting the Public" (CM 965) set out a number of proposals to reform young offender legislation, including new arrangements for the remand of alleged juvenile offenders; extending the jurisdiction of the juvenile court to include those aged 17; and renaming the juvenile court as the Youth Court. At the time this booklet went to print those proposals were being considered in the context of the Criminal Justice Bill.

Conclusion

6.46. While the offending provisions described above remain separate from civil arrangements under the Children Act, it should be borne in mind that for some children a civil disposal (for example, a care order) may be appropriate where a child's offending is a symptom of wider family difficulties. This means early diversion of the child into the civil part of the system before a decision to prosecute is taken. This reinforces the need for close and effective inter-agency co-operation to be established as described in paragraphs 6.6 and 6.9 above.

TRANSITIONAL ARRANGEMENTS

Schedule 14 of the Children Act makes transitional provisions regarding orders made under legislation which is repealed on commencement of the Act. These are outlined below.

Care Orders

Paragraph 15(1) of Schedule 14 lists the orders by virtue of which a child may be in the care of a local authority, and which are subject to the transitional provisions. The Courts and Legal Services Act 1990 extends the list to include any child who is in care by virtue of an order made in the exercise of the High Court's inherent jurisdiction with respect to children (Courts and Legal Services Act 1990, schedule 16 paragraph 33(2)).

On commencement of Part IV of the Children Act, any order made under the provisions listed in paragraph 15(1) of schedule 14 will be deemed to be an order made under section 31 of the Children Act. Apart from some exceptions, any care order which is affected by the transitional provisions will be subject to the same provisions, regulations and guidance as an order made under the Children Act. The exceptions are:

1. Where a child is the subject of a care order by virtue of any of the following provisions:

    section 20(3)(a) or 21(1) of the Children and Young Persons Act 1969; or

    paragraph 7(5)(c)(i) of schedule 5A to the Army Act 1955, schedule 5A to the Air Force Act 1955 or schedule 4A to the Naval Discipline Act 1957,

    the order may last until the child reaches the age of 19, ie., in section 91(12) of the Children Act 'eighteen' must be read as 'nineteen' for these particular cases.

2. Where a child is deemed, by virtue of section 7(3) of Schedule 5A to the Army Act 1955, Schedule 5A to the Air Force Act 1955 or Schedule 4A to the Naval Discipline Act 1957, to be the subject of a care order under the Children and Young Persons Act 1969, the provisions of section 101 of the Children Act (Effect of orders as between England and Wales and Northern Ireland, the Channel Islands or the Isle of Man) do not apply.

3. Where a child is the subject of a deemed care order by virtue of paragraph 15(2)(e) to (h) of schedule 14 and, prior to the commencement of Part IV of the Children Act, a court gave directions:

    under section 4(4)(a) of the Guardianship Act 1973;

    under section 43(5)(a) of the Matrimonial Causes Act 1973; or

    in the exercise of the High Court's inherent jurisdiction with respect to children,

    the directions will continue to have effect until varied or discharged by a court under paragraph 16(5) of schedule 14. But such directions are not to have effect in relation to secure accommodation (this last point is provided for in the Commencement Order).*

Orders for access to a child in care, made under section 12C of the Child Care Act 1980 will, on commencement of Part IV, be treated as contact orders made under section 34 of the Children Act in favour of the person named in the order.

If an access order made under section 12C of the Child Care Act 1980 had, prior to the commencement of Part IV, been suspended by virtue of section 12E of the 1980 Act, the suspending order continues after the commencement of Part IV as originally intended.

---

*Directions concerning approval by the court of secure placements will be treated as having effect under the Secure Accommodation Regulations as the first approval by a court for 3 months from commencement

If access has been refused or terminated and a notice issued under section 12B it is to be treated as a court order under section 34 of the 1989 Act (See Commencement Order transitional provisions).

Supervision Orders

Supervision orders made under section 1(3)(b) of the Children and Young Persons Act 1969, or under section 21(2) of the Children and Young Persons Act 1969, on the discharge of a care order made under section 1(3)(c) of that Act will, on commencement of Part IV, be deemed to be supervision orders made under section 31 of the Children Act. Any requirements as to residence with a named person will continue to have effect unless the court directs otherwise, and any other requirements or directions given by the court or the supervisor will be deemed to have been imposed or given under schedule 3 of the Children Act.

If the supervision order had been in force for more than 6 months prior to the commencement of Part IV, it will end 6 months after the date of commencement unless the court directs that it should end at the end of a different period not exceeding 3 years or it is due to end at an earlier date (either by virtue of section 91 of the Children Act, or because it would already have ended at an earlier date had the Children Act not been passed). Where this is the case (ie., that the order had been in force for more than 6 months) the provisions of paragraph 6 of schedule 3 (Life of a supervision order) do not apply.

If the supervision order had been in force for less than 6 months prior to the commencement of Part IV, section 91 and paragraph 6 of schedule 3 will have effect unless the court directs that the supervision order will cease to have effect at the end of a different period not exceeding 3 years, or the order would already have ended at an earlier date had the Children Act not been passed.

Supervision orders made under the powers listed at paragraph 26(1) of schedule 14 which were made before the commencement of Part IV are *not* deemed to be supervision orders made under section 31, but will continue in force until 1 year after the date of commencement, unless the court directs that it should end before 1 year, or it would already have ended at an earlier date had the Children Act not been passed.

Place of Safety Orders

A place of safety order made under any of the provisions listed in paragraph 27(2) of schedule 14 will continue to have effect as if the Children Act had not been passed. In addition, any enactments repealed by the Children Act shall continue to have effect so far as is necessary for carrying out the place of safety order as if the Children Act had not been passed.

The effect of this is that place of safety orders and detention under section 28 of the Children and Young Persons Act 1969 will continue unaffected by the Children Act until the expiry date which was decided upon by the court when the order was made and in accordance with the provisions of section 28 as to detention.

Any interim order made under section 23(5) of the Children and Young Persons Act 1963 or section 28(6) of the Children and Young Persons Act 1969 will, in the same way, continue to have effect as if the Children Act had not been passed. However, the provision that other repealed enactments will continue in force *does not* apply.

Printed in the United Kingdom for HMSO
Dd 294301, C250, 2/91